*Period photograph, Corcovado viewed from the grounds of the
American Embassy, Courtesy of Escola Alema, Rio de Janeiro*

A JOURNEY IN BRAZIL:
HENRY WASHINGTON HILLIARD
AND THE BRAZILIAN
ANTI-SLAVERY SOCIETY

David I. Durham and Paul M. Pruitt, Jr.

Occasional Publications of the Bounds Law Library
Number Six
University of Alabama School of Law
2008

Bounds Law Library
University of Alabama School of Law
Tuscaloosa, Alabama
2008

Durham, David I.
Pruitt, Paul M., Jr.
    A journey in Brazil: Henry Washington Hilliard and the Brazilian
anti-slavery society / Paul M. Pruitt, Jr. and David I. Durham.

168 pp. (Occasional Publications of the Bounds Law Library).

CONTENTS

ILLUSTRATIONS

PREFACE AND ACKNOWLEDGMENTS

More often than we would like to acknowledge, the experience of North Americans in hemispherical relations has been characterized by arrogance, greed, and an unchecked imperialism that has generated great wealth and property—mostly for North Americans. The perception of Brazil for most Americans has historically been that of an exotic and unknown place. A seventeenth-century European diplomat described the country in familiar terms: "Brazil is an interesting and exotic place, but one that is peripheral to the central issues of international affairs." For most North Americans it is probably still descriptive of their view of Brazil—a perception that really more than any place in South America or the Caribbean basin, Brazil is a mysterious place—peculiar, and a bit scary.

A Journey in Brazil: Henry Washington Hilliard and the Brazilian Anti-Slavery Society explores the nature of one American's experience in the late-nineteenth century as it relates to Brazilians' attempt to eliminate the institution of slavery from their country. Henry Washington Hilliard was a former United States congressman from Alabama, as well as a diplomat, lawyer, professor and author. Hilliard traveled to Brazil as an appointee of Rutherford Hayes' administration to facilitate trade between the United States and Brazil, as well as to offer assistance to Confederate expatriates who had been suffering in Brazil and wished to return. Hilliard left Brazil four years later with the personal

vii

satisfaction that he had been able to contribute to the cause of ending slavery in Brazil.

A collection of edited and introduced documents relating to Hilliard's experience in Brazil, *A Journey in Brazil* offers the reader a glimpse into a North American diplomat's improbable encounter with Brazilian abolition efforts. It offers unique translations of benevolent American diplomacy as well as letters and documents that have never been published. Hilliard's participation—as an antislavery southerner speaking in support of Brazilian abolitionists—represents a remarkable and unique chapter in American diplomatic relations.

The editors' introduction is followed by an essay that describes Hilliard's personal and diplomatic journey, while placing the reproduced letters and historical documents in perspective. The translated and transcribed material is presented with only minimal stylistic and clarifying changes. Well-known Brazilian abolitionist Joaquim Nabuco's letter soliciting Hilliard's assistance is followed by Hilliard's open letter reply, and an original translation of the notable speeches offered at the Brazilian Anti-Slavery Society's banquet that was given in honor of Hilliard's efforts toward abolition. A transcription of the Manifesto of the Brazilian Anti-Slavery Society follows and offers a perspective of Brazilian abolitionists on the topic of slavery and its eventual demise. The manifesto served as a propaganda tool of the society, as well as a blueprint for Hilliard's comments in his open letter to Nabuco which were widely reproduced in the Brazilian press and passionately debated in the Brazilian chamber of deputies.

Editors David I. Durham[1] and Paul M. Pruitt, Jr.[2] would like to thank Dean Kenneth C. Randall and Associate Dean

---

[1] David I. Durham is curator of archival collections at the University of Alabama School of Law and teaches in the history department at the University of Alabama. He is co-editor of, and contributing author to the Occasional Publications of the Bounds Law Library.

James Leonard for their support and encouragement of this project. They thank the staff of the Bounds Law Library for their support and forbearance. They especially thank Peggy Cook for acquiring materials supporting research, Penny Calhoun Gibson for her help with interlibrary loan materials, Jennifer McCracken for graphics assistance, and Ruth Weeks and Julie Kees for advice on cataloging and classification. Also, many thanks to Chuck King and B.J. Harrison from the office of fiscal services. Additional thanks go to Clint Leonard, Brandon Wooten, Ashley Flubacher, and Adam Eason for research and production assistance. Thanks to Kim Spencer, Bulk Mail Coordinator at University Printing, and to Teresa Golson of the Faculty Resource Center for her exceptional photographic imaging.

Many thanks to law professor and historian Alfred L. Brophy of the University of Alabama School of Law for his encouragement and interest in this work. For good suggestions concerning research on Dom Pedro II in Brazil, the editors thank Roderick Barman, professor emeritus in the history department of the University of British Columbia. Thanks to Rickie Louise Brunner at the Alabama Department of Archives and History; Dwayne Cox, head of special collections and archives, Auburn University; and archivist Mary Ann Pickard, commission on archives and history, Alabama-West Florida Methodist Conference, Huntingdon College Library.

It is with pleasure we thank a number of people in Brazil for their help with this project. At the Fundação Biblioteca Nacional in Rio de Janeiro, we wish to thank Anna Maria Naldi, Divisão Obras Gerais; Vera Lucia Miranda Faillace, chefe da divisão de manuscritos; Monica Carneiro Alves, Departamento Iconografia; and special thanks to Filippa

---

[2] Paul M. Pruitt, Jr. is collection development and special collections librarian at the University of Alabama School of Law. He is co-editor of, and contributing author to the Occasional Publications of the Bounds Law Library.

Faria. Thanks to fellow researcher Thais Rezende at the Biblioteca Nacional; and we thank Diego Martinez, super-intendente adm. e financeiro at Escola Alemã Corcovado, for his hospitality at the former American embassy site. We thank Pamela Howard-Reguindin, field director for the Library of Congress office at the American consulate, Rio de Janeiro. At the Universidade Federal do Rio de Janeiro, we thank Carlos Fico, coordenador programa de Pós-Graduação em História Social, for his help and we extend much gratitude to William Martins for his support. For her invaluable help, patience, insight, and keen research skills, a special thanks to Amina Maria Figueroa Vergara. In Recife we thank Samantha Nicoleli, chefe de serviços, Centro de Documentação de Estudos da História Brasileira, for her help with Joaquim Nabuco's letters. Especially for her patience and assistance with long hours of translations we warmly thank Kely Melo.

Henry Washington Hilliard c. 1890
From Politics and Pen Pictures at Home and Abroad

INTRODUCTION

AMICUS CURIAE: HENRY W. HILLIARD'S VIEW OF SLAVERY

On an October day in 1877, United States ambassador Henry Washington Hilliard arrived at Rio de Janeiro. The voyage from Bordeaux had been pleasant and safe, both matters of concern for the sixty-one year old diplomat. As his ship approached the South American coast he had his first glimpse of tropical foliage. Of the scenery near Rio he would write that it "transcended anything in sublimity that I had seen in any country."[1] As his biographer David Durham observes, it was clear that Hilliard "reveled in the beginning of such an exotic adventure."[2]

Such exuberance may have been unusual in an elderly man, but Hilliard's emotions were very much in tune with the spirit of his times. Anglo-Americans of the nineteenth and early twentieth centuries prized exploration and exotic scenery, viewing tropical lands as laboratories in which northern ideas (science, progress) could be tested in environments of great natural abundance. During this age of adventure and capitalism, a succession of visitors exclaim-

---

[1] Henry W. Hilliard, *Politics and Pen Pictures at Home and Abroad* (New York: G.P. Putnam's Sons, 1892), 361, 362.
[2] David I. Durham, "Henry Washington Hilliard: 'A Story of Plebeians and Patricians'" (Ph.D. dissertation, University of Alabama, 2005), 213. Also see, David I. Durham, *A Southern Moderate in Radical Times: Henry Washington Hilliard, 1808-1892* (Baton Rouge: Louisiana State University Press, 2008).

ed over Brazil's natural beauty, meanwhile interpreting Brazilian culture in light of their own devices and desires.[3]

Thus Hilliard was one of many visiting strangers, diplomats, and explorers, all of more or less interest to their hosts and to modern scholars. Yet Hilliard stands out from Brazil's other guests because he was both willing and uniquely qualified to enter that nation's public dialog. In matters pertaining to race and slavery—hotly debated in Brazil before and after his arrival—Hilliard could speak authoritatively as a former slaveholder, but likewise as a man who had been a conservative critic of slavery and was now the representative of a great emancipationist power. This essay is intended to provide context for Hilliard's attitudes toward race and slavery, and to introduce David Durham's biographical and critical narrative.

In some respects, Hilliard was a conventional and competent diplomat, a thoroughgoing American imperialist. A former Whig congressman who had also served (1842-1844) as minister to Belgium, he was a dedicated servant of his country's economic and political interests.[4] On the other hand, Hilliard—born in North Carolina,

---

[3] Readers may want to consider the works of such scientific conquistadors as Louis Agassiz, who headed the 1865 "Thayer Expedition;" see Louis and Elizabeth Cabot Cary Agassiz, *A Journey in Brazil* (Boston: Ticknor and Fields, 1868); see also Louis Menand, *The Metaphysical Club: A Story of Ideas in America* (New York: Farrar, Straus, and Giroux, 2001), 117-148, discussing both Agassiz and the youthful William James, who was a member of the expedition. Also enlightening are two very different works published almost simultaneously a generation later. For the work of a distinguished political scientist and British diplomat, see James Bryce's *South America: Observations and Impressions* (New York: Macmillan Company, 1912). Arthur Conan Doyle's *The Lost World* (New York: Hodder and Stoughton, George Moran Company, 1912) is a Darwinian fiction in which explorers discover a Brazilian plateau populated by dinosaurs, primitive tribesmen, and even more primitive ape-men.
[4] For Hilliard's successful negotiation of a trademark treaty, see Hilliard, *Politics and Pen Pictures*, 373-376.

2

educated in South Carolina, long-time resident of Alabama and Georgia—was no arrogant North American. Rather he was a man of sympathetic culture and inquiring mind, an antebellum Southerner who had excelled at diverse careers: professor, Methodist clergyman, editor, lawyer, and politician. A reluctant Confederate soldier, he was well acquainted with the consequences of military defeat (an atypical experience for non-Confederate Americans) and with the weight of collective guilt over the South's "peculiar institution."[5] For Hilliard, who had warmly embraced service in the court of Brazil's emperor Dom Pedro II, the assignment was a blessed chance for professional and personal redemption.

Despite striking successes in several fields Hilliard had been haunted by a sense of failure, by what Durham sums up as a "lifetime of personal and professional disappointments." To an extent his troubled self-image was the product of temperament. A true child of the perpetual motion machine that was nineteenth-century America, Hilliard "did not really find his place anywhere." Instead, "his life was spent in the restless pursuit of some great accomplishment, some defining moment."[6] His vision of that shining moment was the product of Classical and rhetorical training. Early in life he took the Athenian orator Demosthenes as his model, hoping by means of eloquence to move the people toward peace and freedom.[7]

The notion of serving as a type of democratic lawgiver was both Classical and Romantic, and was in either case a

---

[5] On these points, see C. Vann Woodward, "The Irony of Southern History," in *The Burden of Southern History*, revised edition (Baton Rouge: Louisiana State University Press, 1968), 187-211.

[6] Durham, "Henry Washington Hilliard," quoted passages on 243, 261.

[7] For Demosthenes, see Arthur Hugh Clough, editor, *Plutarch: The Lives of the Noble Greeks and Romans,* translated by John Dryden (reprint of 1864 edition; New York: Modern Library, [1932]), 1022-1040; for the paired biography of Cicero, see *ibid.*, 1041-1072.

dangerous precedent. Demosthenes and Cicero each died at the hands of tyrants, after all, and Romantic heroes were apt to perish Byron-like in turbulent waters. Yet the youthful Hilliard piled Christian fervor upon Classical training and Romantic inclinations, and such was his faith—in progress, in human goodness—that he could brush aside consideration of dark forces. "Never again," he told the University of Alabama's Erosophic Society in 1832, "shall a senate hall bristle with bayonets; the empire of mind is established, and henceforth nations are to be ranked, not according to their *physical*, but their *moral* strength."[8]

As a Whig politician, Hilliard favored Henry Clay's "American System," a loosely joined group of enactments and proposals that embraced protective tariffs, central banking, and government-backed internal improvements. The rock upon which Hilliard (and ultimately, the Whig Party) foundered was that of slavery. From the late 1840s to the outbreak of the Civil War, issues of slavery—its morality or immorality, its spread into western territories, the extent to which the Federal government could or couldn't interfere with state laws protecting it—came to dominate national politics. Most white Southerners, including Whigs, would not accept the idea of a society based on racial equality.[9] That way, they were convinced, lay a southern-American version of the Haitian revolution, complete with racial violence and political disarray.[10]

---

[8] Henry W. Hilliard, *An Address Delivered Before the Erosophic Society, At Its First Anniversary* (Tuscaloosa: Wiley, M'Guire and Henry, Printers, 1832), 4.

[9] See Hilliard, *Politics and Pen Pictures*, 352, for his remark: "I firmly believe that the supremacy of the white race is absolutely essential to the existence of our social system in these Southern States."

[10] For the deep impression made upon white Southerners by events in Haiti, 1791-1804, see Michael O'Brien, *Conjectures of Order: Intellectual Life and the American South* (Chapel Hill: University of North Carolina Press, 2004), I: 207-209.

Fearful of Federal power, Southerners embraced states rights principles so totally that many Southern Whigs, including Hilliard, joined Democrats in making slaveholding a sacred right under the Constitution. Eventually, as Northern opinion solidified into a determination to limit slavery's expansion and generally to condemn the institution, Hilliard and other one-time stalwarts of the Whig Party would acquiesce in secession. Some of them, like Hilliard and his contemporary Thomas Hill Watts, would perform valuable service for the Confederacy. The breakup of the Union was utterly distasteful to Hilliard. Psychologically the worst of it may have been that his political rival and near neighbor, William Lowndes Yancey, had seized the mantle of Demosthenes, rallying white Southerners with speech after speech—philippics in the truest sense.[11]

But for Hilliard the ultimate irony of the slaveholder's revolution was that though he had defended slaveholders' rights, he wasn't comfortable with slavery. A number of his Whig allies shared this state of unease, as well as a few Democrats. These were conservative critics of the peculiar institution, men who expected, even hoped, that some combination of climate, economics, and moral suasion would eventually undermine it.[12] But they were always a small minority in the South, and by the 1850s the pressure

---

[11] Durham, "Henry Washington Hilliard," 103-107, 116-118, 127, 134-135, 138-139, 143-150, 151-164, 171-191. During this time Hilliard frequently declared his love for the Union, warning that the antislavery movement would destroy it. For Hilliard's service as Confederate commissioner to Tennessee and commander of troops, see below. Watts, another of Yancey's respected opponents, would serve as Attorney General of the Confederacy and as governor of Alabama.

[12] For the analogous case of Francis Lieber, a famous political economist who shared Hilliard's conviction that slavery was doomed, and who like Hilliard was haunted by a sense of personal failure, see O'Brien, *Conjectures of Order*, I: 73-87. From 1835 to 1856 Lieber was a professor at South Carolina College, Hilliard's alma mater.

of events was such that they did not dare to speak out. Perhaps they were wise to be crypto-abolitionists. After John Brown's October 1859 raid in Virginia, Southern communities enforced proslavery orthodoxy by methods that were little short of revolutionary.[13] In April 1861 Hilliard himself served on a committee of six, secretly chartered by the Montgomery, Alabama, city government. Their task: to investigate disloyal remarks allegedly made by schoolmaster W.H. Wilkinson. The committee cleared the teacher's name, but could just as easily have had him whipped and expelled from town.[14]

It was clear that neither personal prominence nor distance offered protection from witch-hunters. John A. Campbell of Mobile, an associate justice of the U.S. Supreme Court, had raised eyebrows a decade earlier (1847-1851) by a series of articles in which he called for reforms in the legal regime of slavery. While he favored enhancing slaves' human rights, he certainly had not called for abolition. Nonetheless his Southern allegiance was suspect, and when he remained in Washington after Alabama seceded (seeking to mediate a peaceful transfer of

---

[13] For the shrinking influence of reasoned antislavery arguments in the south, see Elizabeth Fox-Genovese and Eugene Genovese, *The Mind of the Master Class: History and Faith in the Southern Slaveholders' Worldview* (New York: Cambridge university Press, 2005), 229-240; and Clement Eaton, *The Freedom-of-Thought Struggle in the Old South* (New York: Harper and Row, 1964).

[14] See the Montgomery *Advertiser*, March 23, 24, 26, 30, April 4, 17, 18, 1861, for a whipping-and-expulsion in nearby Lowndes County and for coverage of the Montgomery investigation. Margaret M. Storey, *Loyalty and Loss: Alabama's Unionists in the Civil War and Reconstruction* (Baton Rouge: Louisiana State University Press, 2004) 63, asserts that during the "secession crisis," Alabama "had seen a marked increase in its number of operative vigilance committees, many of which bullied pro-Union men."

Federal properties, notably Fort Sumter) he was branded a traitor in his hometown of Mobile.[15]

High-placed or lowly, it seems that quite a few Alabamians paid a price for the luxury of voicing their thoughts. But what would Hilliard and like-minded Alabamians have said, had they been freer to speak their minds? First, in common with all but a few proslavery ideologues, they would have agreed with Justice John J. Ormond of the Alabama Supreme Court that African American slaves were "intellectual, moral beings" capable of "attachments of the strongest kind."[16] Second, though like most white Alabamians they believed that the majority of slaves were well treated, they were aware that legally all slaves were both human beings and chattel property—a status inconsistent with contemporary notions of human dignity and rights. As Hilliard would write of Brazilian slaves, they were "ground between the upper and the nether mill-stone."[17]

In fact the American definition of slavery was a recipe for exploitation and for the triumph of "the coarser and meaner lusts," as Hilliard would admit in Brazil, over "the better qualities of human nature."[18] Paternalistic slave

---

[15] Robert Saunders, Jr., *John Archibald Campbell, Southern Moderate* (Tuscaloosa: University of Alabama Press, 1997), 57-68, 137-144, 146-153, and (for Campbell's later Confederate service as Assistant Secretary of War) 153-160. See also Thomas C. DeLeon, *Four Years in Rebel Capitals* (reprint of 1892 edition; Spartanburg, South Carolina, Reprint Company, 1975), 55, describing the "hisses and execrations" that greeted mention of Campbell's name at a mass meeting in Mobile.

[16] Quoted in William E. Wiethoff, *A Peculiar Humanism: The Judicial Advocacy of Slavery in High Courts of the Old South, 1820-1850* (Athens, Georgia: University of Georgia Press, 1996), 66, 67 (from two decisions). Ormond was one of Alabama's most notable antebellum jurists.

[17] Hilliard, *Politics and Pen Pictures*, 398.

[18] See Henry W. Hilliard to Joaquim Nabuco, October 25, 1880, Hilliard Correspondence, *Fundação Joaquim Nabuco*, Recife, Brazil, reprinted below.

owners like Hilliard or his former colleague Henry Tutwiler could persuade themselves that their own establishments were organic communities of white and black, in which hierarchy did not preclude respect and affection.[19] However, such men were well acquainted with an alternative scenario, the predominant one according to Thomas Jefferson, in which the master-slave relationship corrupts both parties, turning masters into tyrants and slaves into their covert or (terrifyingly) overt enemies.[20]

Apart from moral objections to slavery as a destroyer of souls black and white, Hilliard and his cohorts understood that slavery was a barrier to their own participation in the transoceanic world. Hilliard was happily at home among cultivated, well-to-do people in Boston or Paris.[21] Yet as early as 1849 he was ready to admit on the floor of Congress: "There is a domestic institution in the South

---

[19] For Hilliard's self-assessment ("No man is more sincerely the friend of the Negro than myself; my life has shown it") see Hilliard, *Politics and Pen Pictures*, 352; for Hilliard as owner of fourteen slaves, see Durham, "Henry Washington Hilliard," 135 n. 153. Henry Tutwiler, who had served with Hilliard on the faculty of the University of Alabama, was headmaster of the famous Greene Springs School and owner of twenty slaves. See Paul M. Pruitt, Jr., "The Education of Julia Tutwiler: Prelude to a Life of Reform," *Alabama Review*, 46 (July 1993), 202-210. In a letter to James G. Birney, August 20, 1832, in Dwight L. Dumond, editor, *Letters of James Gillespie Birney, 1831-1857* (reprint of 1938 edition; Gloucester, Massachusetts: Peter Smith, 1966), I: 17-20, Tutwiler remarks of slavery that "almost all the moral and political evil in our Country may be traced to this fruitful source." Tutwiler had known Thomas Jefferson personally while a student at the University of Virginia.

[20] For Jefferson on slavery, see Merrill D. Peterson, editor, *Thomas Jefferson, Writings* (New York: Library of America, 1984), 269, 288-289.

[21] Hilliard was a talented linguist, fluent in French and a student of Italian. Consider his translation of Alessandro Verri's *Roman Nights: Or, The Tomb of the Scipios* (Philadelphia: J. Ball, 1850).

which in some sort insulates us from all mankind."[22] A challenge that faces post-colonial societies—namely, that of maintaining cultural relations with metropolitan powers while applying older concepts in self-consciously independent settings—was growing more difficult for the Southerners, even as they declared their cultural independence from the Northern states.[23]

The problem went beyond economic matters, beyond J.A. Campbell's conviction, in the words of his biographer, that slavery kept the South in a state of "perpetual commercial limbo."[24] Whiggish intellectuals were distressed at the prospect of guilt by association with a regime that was condemned, as the Alabama prison reformer Benjamin F. Porter wrote in 1865, by the "whole civilized world."[25] But no one had summed up the dangers to the Southern status quo better than Hilliard in the 1849 speech already quoted. "The tide has been rising higher and higher," he had continued, "until, sir, we begin to feel the spray breaking over the very embankments which surround us." He rounded out the metaphor by concluding that the South's dykes could "hardly protect the habitations of man" from seas of change.[26]

In his end-of-life memoir *Politics and Pen Pictures*, Hilliard does not reveal the extent of his suffering during the deluge. Yet Durham's writings show us that Hilliard was better at raising troops than at commanding them, and that politically he was reduced to sending letters of advice. After the surrenders of 1865, much of his energy would be

---

[22] Henry W. Hilliard, "Governments for the New Territories—The North and the South," in Hilliard, *Speeches and Addresses* (New York: Harper and Brothers, 1855), 214.

[23] O'Brien, *Conjectures of Order*, I: 2-5.

[24] Saunders, *John Archibald Campbell*, 58.

[25] Paul M. Pruitt, Jr., "An Antebellum Law Reformer: Passages in the Life of Benjamin F. Porter," *Gulf Coast Historical Review*, 11 (Fall 1995), 46.

[26] Hilliard, "Governments for the New Territories," 215.

focused on obtaining the pardons necessary for a return to public life. Thanks to Durham's research we also know that Hilliard's image as a man of honor—essential to participation in either law or politics—was in jeopardy during these years. His first wife had died in June 1862. A hasty marriage to his wife's best friend had caused a scandal that drove him from Alabama to Georgia, and brought an end to his career in the pulpit. By 1867 Hilliard had completed his undoing from the standpoint of white Southern opinion by declaring himself a Republican, thereby becoming what most ex-Confederates called a Scalawag.[27]

President Rutherford B. Hayes, on the lookout for suitably qualified white Southerners, interrupted Hilliard's freefall by offering him the Brazil mission. As Durham reveals in his narrative below, Hilliard viewed diplomacy as an opportunity to reassert himself as a public figure—specifically to exert himself as a righteous agent wielding the power of a reunified United States. As Durham shows, Hilliard studied hard for his Brazilian assignment, acquainting himself with the young giant's difficulties.[28] Like the U.S., Brazil was wasted by war[29] and troubled by labor and social disputes. Unlike the U.S., Brazil was still encumbered by the divisive issue of slavery. Despite the 1871 "Free Birth" law or "Lei do Ventre Livre" that had committed the imperial government to gradual emancipation of 1.5 million slaves, the institution's end was neither close nor certain.[30] What a delicious irony, Hilliard must have

---

[27] See Durham, "Henry Washington Hilliard," 185-210.

[28] *Ibid.*, 221.

[29] In Brazil's case, the War of the Triple Alliance (1864-1870); for a brief summary, see G. Pope Atkins, *Latin American and the Caribbean in the International System*, 4th edition (Boulder, Colorado: Westview Press, 1999), 321.

[30] Robert Conrad, "Translator's Introduction," to Joaquim Nabuco, *Abolitionism: The Brazilian Antislavery Struggle* (translation of the 1883 edition of *O Abolicionismo*; Urbana, Illinois: University of Illinois Press, 1977), xvii.

thought, that the evil regime of slavery—derailer of his former life—should now present him with an opportunity for greatness.[31]

Hilliard's antislavery pronouncements of October and November 1880 were the greatest accomplishments of his post-bellum life. They were facilitated by his friendship with Joaquim Nabuco, who though he was a descendant of slaveholding planters followed a path marked out by his father, a leader of Brazil's Liberal party and an author of the 1871 emancipation law. Nabuco was still young; he turned 31 in 1880, the year he founded the Brazilian Antislavery Society. But he had already displayed varied gifts as poet, polemicist, editor, lawyer, and legislator. He easily captured Hilliard's sympathy, partly because he opposed violence as a means of securing freedom for the slaves, preferring "the abolition of Wilberforce, Lamartine, and Garrison" to that of "Cataline or Spartacus or John Brown."[32] The young legislator also impressed Hilliard as an effective organizer and legislative leader. Most of all,

---

[31] Along related paths of irony, Hilliard would be instrumental in relieving the suffering of many "Confederados." These were Confederates who had fled the post-bellum south, tempted by offers of government-subsidized lands and hopeful of launching a new cotton kingdom. For more information see Durham, "Henry Washington Hilliard," 230-234; Cyrus B. Dawsey and James M. Dawsey, editors, *The Confederados: Old South Immigrants in Brazil* (Tuscaloosa: University of Alabama Press, 1995); Eugene C. Harter, *The Lost Colony of the Confederacy* (Jackson: University Press of Mississippi, 1985); and below.

[32] See Conrad, "Translator's Introduction," xii-xxii; and Nabuco, *Abolitionism*, 24 (quoted passage). The references are to William Wilberforce of England, Alphonse Lamartine of France, and William Lloyd Garrison of the U.S., who are held up as nonviolent reformers in comparison to the Roman demagogue Cataline, the slave rebel Spartacus, and the American firebrand John Brown.

Hilliard saw Nabuco as a younger, freer version of himself.[33]

Invited to comment on the effects of emancipation in his native South, Hilliard responded eagerly, first by an open letter to Nabuco and subsequently as guest of honor at an Antislavery Society banquet.[34] Like a goodly number of former Confederates he was ready to proclaim his pleasure over slavery's demise.[35] Refurbishing the cryptoabolitionist arguments against slavery, Hilliard praised the immediate, uncompensated abolition of slavery in America, despite its accompaniment of war and social dislocation, as an act in accord with the moral order of the universe. Hilliard was inclined to doubt the wisdom of enfranchising a people without previous experience of participation in civic life. Yet he praised the freedmen for their nonviolence, diligence, and reliability, their success in acquiring property, and their willingness to work toward community with their former masters. Lapsing into an early version of New South boosterism, Hilliard declared that the South had never been so prosperous, so peaceful, or so attractive to immigrants.[36]

As for emancipation in Brazil, Hilliard gave his blessing to the gradualist approach. Yet he urged that all slaves be freed within seven years, a proposal that touched off a political controversy. Proslavery legislators accused him, not without reason, of interfering in national affairs. The

---

[33] Hilliard, *Politics and Pen Pictures*, 381; and see below. See also Durham, "Henry Washington Hilliard," 240-242.

[34] Hilliard, *Politics and Pen Pictures*, 394-398.

[35] See Mary Gorton McBride and Ann Mathison McLaurin, *Randall Lee Gibson of Louisiana: Confederate General and New South Reformer* (Baton Rouge: Louisiana State University Press, 2007), 158.

[36] See Hilliard to Nabuco, October 25, 1880; and Hilliard's *Hotel dos Estrangeiros* (banquet) speech of November 20, 1880, both below. For Hilliard's "New South" attitudes see below; in general, see Paul M. Gaston, *The New South Creed: A Study in Southern Mythmaking* (New York: Alfred A. Knopf, 1970).

danger was that the imperial government might repudiate him, despite his earnest efforts to ingratiate himself with the Court. In the end, the emperor's counselor defended the American ambassador before the chamber of deputies, offering the royal opinion that Hilliard had commented on slavery in his private capacity only. Meanwhile Nabuco's circle benefited from the continued momentum of the issue, and Hilliard enjoyed the little tempest to the full. "I became the central figure of the agitation," he would write, "and I was observed in every circle."[37]

After enjoying his victory for six months, Hilliard resigned his post and voyaged to Europe (where he had deposited his family). He returned home to a South quite different from the one he had described—one in which prosperity and racial harmonies were harder to find with each passing year. Settling in Atlanta in a house once occupied by the celebrated New South journalist Henry W. Grady,[38] he dabbled at practicing law and wrote *Politics and Pen Pictures*, which was published in 1892, the year of his death. This memoir shows plainly that Hilliard was a representative of what historian Carl Degler has called the "Other South," a South that was not secessionist, not filled with sectional hatreds or driven by an ignorant, hysterical racism.[39] As such Hilliard was the polar opposite of Southern stereotypes.

It would be interesting to know whether the Classically inclined Hilliard was an admirer of British Poet-Laureate Alfred Tennyson, specifically of Tennyson's 1842 poem "Ulysses." In the poem the aged Greek hero, home from his long odyssey, discovers that he "cannot rest from travel." Having enjoyed a life spent "always roaming with a hungry

---

[37] Hilliard, *Politics and Pen Pictures*, 397-402, quoted passage on 397.

[38] Durham, "Henry Washington Hilliard," 257. Appropriately, the house was named "New South."

[39] See Carl N. Degler, *The Other South: Southern Dissenters in the Nineteenth Century* (New York: Harper and Row, 1974).

heart," he has decided to seek adventure one last time, telling his elderly shipmates that "tis not too late to seek a new world." Obviously Hilliard did not imitate Ulysses' plan of sailing on to a certain if glamorous death. Still, readers of *Politics and Pen Pictures* cannot help but see Hilliard's voyage to Brazil as a heroic endeavor. And there is one more similarity between Hilliard and Tennyson's protagonist—both were delighted to declare that they had been everywhere the choice companions of the good and the great. Throughout his memoir Hilliard seems to be saying, like Ulysses: "Much have I seen and known; cities of men and manners, climates, councils, governments, myself not least, but honored of them all."[40]

---

[40] For "Ulysses" see Lionel Trilling and Harold Bloom, editors, *Victorian Prose and Poetry* (New York: Oxford University Press, 1973), 416-418. Hilliard and Tennyson were in fact close contemporaries. Hilliard, born on August 4, 1808, was a year older than Tennyson, born August 6, 1809. Hilliard died on December 17, 1892, surviving by a little more than two months Tennyson, who had died on October 9.

Former site of the American Embassy, Escola Alema, Rio de Janeiro
Photograph by David I. Durham, June 2006

16

AN IMPROBABLE JOURNEY[1]

On a pleasant spring evening in 1880 in the Rio de Janeiro neighborhood of Cattete, United States minister to Brazil, Henry Washington Hilliard rose from his seat in the opulent grand salon of the *Hotel dos Estrangeiros* to speak on the topic of Brazilian slavery. Receiving a hero's introduction, Hilliard spoke to the fifty Brazilian abolitionists and statesmen who were gathered at the banquet honoring his involvement in the Brazilian anti-slavery effort. Hilliard's speech acknowledged his appreciation for the opportunity to speak out in support of the effort to abolish slavery in Brazil. In simplest terms, Hilliard's odyssey represents one man's attempt at redemption

---

[1] *A Journey in Brazil* describes Harvard naturalist, Louis Agassiz's year in Brazil and his change of scientific focus from Old World Europe to South America. His volume not only highlights a naturalist's view of Brazil during the mid-nineteenth century, but also offers a narrative that provides vivid and romantic descriptions of the country and its inhabitants. Agassiz and his wife received assistance from among others, American Minister James Watson Webb, and Emperor Dom Pedro II who showed great interest in the couple's scientific activities and expressed kinship with their scientific endeavors. Among their social observations were comments concerning the effect of emancipation in the United States on the issue of slavery in Brazil. Professor and Mrs. Louis Agassiz, *A Journey in Brazil* (Boston: Ticknor and Fields, 1868), v-viii, and *passim*. For a comprehensive study of Hilliard's life and career, see David I. Durham, *A Southern Moderate in Radical Times: Henry Washington Hilliard, 1808-1892* (Baton Rouge: Louisiana State University Press, 2008), or David I. Durham, "Henry Washington Hilliard: 'A Story of Plebeians and Patricians'" (Ph.D. dissertation, University of Alabama, 2005).

through his participation in the Brazilian anti-slavery cause. Whether through Divine Providence, or as the result of decisions made by an ambitious, talented, and ultimately flawed individual, Hilliard's path was a mixture of both significant accomplishments and remarkable failures.

Hilliard was emblematic of the elite lawyer-statesman of the nineteenth century, and fulfilled his role as a privileged member of the ruling class with an almost classical sense of public duty that was instilled in him as a young man. Even so, he consistently struggled with a strong sense of responsibility toward the less advantaged elements of society. To better understand the significance of this remarkable celebration honoring the former United States congressman and lawyer from Alabama, it is necessary to look briefly at the improbable journey that brought him to Brazil.

Born on August 4, 1808, at Fayetteville, Cumberland County, North Carolina, Henry Washington Hilliard was the son of William and Mary Hilliard.[2] Although Hilliard had a number of relatives in the northern counties of Edgecombe and Northampton, North Carolina, his mother and father moved the family to Columbia, South Carolina when Henry Hilliard was an infant. Little is known about Hilliard's life in Columbia until he was admitted to South Carolina College at fifteen.[3]

---

[2] Henry W. Hilliard records at the Commission on Archives and History, Alabama-West Florida Conference, United Methodist Church, Huntingdon College Library, Montgomery, Alabama.

[3] South Carolina College after a long period of reconstitution following the Civil War made the transition to the University of South Carolina. For South Carolina College and the University of South Carolina, see Daniel Walker Hollis, *University of South Carolina, Volume I, South Carolina College* (Columbia: University of South Carolina Press, 1951); *University of South Carolina, Volume II, College to University* (Columbia: University of South Carolina Press, 1956); and M. La-Borde, *History of the South Carolina College, From Its Incorporation December 19, 1801, to November 25, 1857, Including Sketches of Its Presidents and Professors* (Columbia: Peter B. Glass, 1859).

When Hilliard arrived on campus, the college was in a transitional period. Its first president, Jonathan Maxcy, had been a beloved but nondescript Baptist minister who had mostly avoided disagreements. His successor, Thomas Cooper, thrived on controversy, wrote voluminously, and became a nationally-renowned intellectual figure. It was during Cooper's tenure that academics at the college became significantly tougher.[4] Of Hilliard's professors at South Carolina College, reputedly the most dynamic and influential was president Cooper who taught chemistry and politics. the class that perhaps offered the most interest for Hilliard was the course in Political Economy. Here Cooper exposed his young and impressionable students to the principles of *laissez-faire* economics as expounded by notable economic theorists such as Adam Smith, David Ricardo, and James Mill, and more importantly, the doctrine of States' Rights of which Cooper was a radical champion, earning him the moniker of "Schoolmaster of States' Rights."[5] Maximilian LaBorde, a student during the 1820s, provides insight into Cooper's teaching ability:

> He had mingled intimately with the most
> remarkable men of the Old and the New World, and
> had been an eye-witness of some of the most
> stirring and interesting events recorded in history.
> He knew Fox, and Pitt, and Sheridan, and Erskine
> and Burke, and would tell of the impression made
> upon him when he witnessed those mighty efforts
> which have shed such glory upon the authors and

---

[4] For comparisons of Jonathan Maxcy and Thomas Cooper and the tightening of standards at South Carolina College, see Hollis, *South Carolina College*, I: 77-83; and LaBorde, *History of the South Carolina College*, 127-137.

[5] See Hollis, *South Carolina College*, I: 81-82. Hilliard, a devoted Whig, apparently was not influenced positively by Cooper's arguments for the principles of *laissez-faire* economics.

their country. With Watt he had gone to Paris during the French Revolution, and had been closeted with Robespierre, Petion, and other members of the Jacobin Club. Coming to America in 1792, he made the acquaintance of the great men of the Revolution, and throwing himself actively into the cause of Jeffersonian democracy, was admitted to terms of intimacy with its leaders. He turned all his knowledge into account. With wonderful art he could weave a dinner with Priestley, a glass of wine with Robespierre, a supper with the Brissotians, or a race for the Convention against the Duke of Orleans, into a lecture.[6]

Cooper's ideas and teaching greatly influenced the careers of many future legal, judicial, and political leaders, though interestingly enough, his students embraced diverse political positions. Nullifiers, secessionists, Unionists, and moderates had all been influenced by his teaching. In the class of 1820 was the future radical Calhounite and Alabama Senator Dixon Hall Lewis, as well as Richard Yeaden, the pro-Whig editor of the *Charleston Courier*.[7]

---

[6] LaBorde, *History of the South Carolina College*, 171. Indeed his students were not alone in their perception of Cooper's abilities. Thomas Jefferson wrote a letter to Cooper in 1823 that included the compliment, "no man living cherishes a higher estimation of your worth, talents and information." Thomas Jefferson, *The Works of Thomas Jefferson* (New York: G.P. Putnam's Sons, 1904), 13: 329.

[7] LaBorde, *History of the South Carolina College*, 266. Moderates were graduated after 1825; however, the balance of ideas had shifted toward much stronger beliefs in the doctrine of States' Rights for the majority of the future leaders of the state, and nationalists such as Hilliard were scarce. Hilliard, of course, did not strictly qualify as a Cooper disciple, but even so, it appears that his moderate views developed more fully after leaving South Carolina College, most likely as the result of his association with tutor, friend, former nullifier, and Whig, William Campbell Preston. For William Campbell Preston, *see Biographical Directory of the United States Congress*; Ralph T. Eubanks, "An

Hilliard offered further proof that moderates as well as the radical southern nationalists known as fire-eaters emerged from Cooper's classes.[8] In addition to his course work, Hilliard developed what would become keen oratorical skills as the result of his experience with the literary societies at the college. These groups provided important training outside the classroom for ambitious young men. A mastery of elocution was considered to be an essential element of a superior college education in a society that placed a high value on the persuasiveness of the spoken word.[9] Oratory was a required skill for the successful nineteenth-century politician, especially in the South, and was equally essential to a lucrative legal career.[10] It was through his membership in the Euphradian Literary Society that Hilliard gained experience debating some of the most controversial subjects of the period such as slavery and emancipation, international relations, and the constitutional role of government.[11]

Historical and Rhetorical Study of the Speaking of William C. Preston" (Dissertation, University of Florida, 1957); and William C. Preston, *The Reminiscences of William C. Preston, Edited by Minnie Clare Yarborough* (Chapel Hill: The University of North Carolina Press, 1933).

[8] Hollis, *South Carolina College*, I: 266. Just as politician and historian Edward McCrady, Jr. held onto his South Carolina conservative philosophy and pre-war belief system long after the war, Hilliard as a moderate (or even liberal figure by many Carolinians' standards) also remained true to his pre-war philosophy—even exploring it further in the post-war period. For McCrady and post-war beliefs and philosophy, see Charles J. Holden, *In the Great Maelstrom: Conservatives in Post-Civil War South Carolina* (Columbia: University of South Carolina Press, 2002).

[9] Preston, *The Reminiscences of William C. Preston*, 6.

[10] See, Hollis, *South Carolina College*, I: 230. So strong was the sense of importance of spoken skills at the college, Daniel Hollis in his history of the college and university devoted a chapter to the idea that he described as the "Cult of Oratory." See Hollis, I: 230-254.

[11] LaBorde, *History of the South Carolina College*, 427-428; and Hollis, *South Carolina College*, I: 234-242.

At the age of eighteen, Hilliard graduated from South Carolina College joining an elite group of twenty-eight young men from an institution that educated some of South Carolina's most prominent families.[12] Legal study was a natural choice for a young man interested in politics and Hilliard focused his attention to the field of law. His experience at South Carolina College had uniquely prepared him for his future roles as lawyer, professor, politician, and diplomat, and Hilliard ambitiously anticipated his professional life. Throughout the early nineteenth century, the study of law was commonly pursued through traditional law-office apprenticeships and promising young students were chosen by judges or well-respected senior lawyers to "read law" in their offices. Through the study of select cases and legal works an apprentice would gain the necessary knowledge to pass examination and be admitted to the bar.[13] It was within this system that Hilliard received his legal education, remaining at Columbia, South Carolina for two years studying law in the office of William Campbell Preston, with whom

---

[12] LaBorde, *History of the South Carolina College*, 442.

[13] David I. Durham and Paul M. Pruitt, Jr., *Wade Keyes' Introductory Lecture to the Montgomery Law School: Legal Education in Mid-Nineteenth Century Alabama* (Tuscaloosa: University of Alabama School of Law, 2001), 1-2. Throughout the nineteenth century, legal training in America underwent dramatic changes in both structure and method. The study of the law moved from apprenticeships such as Hilliard's to the college and university systems that developed shortly after Hilliard's study. By the late 1860s, the method of teaching the "science of the law" by tracing the historical development of legal doctrines through the analysis of cases was introduced by Christopher Columbus Langdell at the Harvard Law School and soon became the standard approach to legal study. See Lawrence Friedman, *A History of American Law* (New York: Simon and Schuster, 1973); and for the development of legal education in America and the move away from the more casual and democratic apprenticeship system, see Robert Stevens, *Law School: Legal Education in America from the 1850s to the 1980s* (Chapel Hill: The University of North Carolina Press, 1983).

Hilliard would develop a life-long friendship.[14] Even though his interest in law would become secondary to his political career, Hilliard became a skillful attorney. After two years under Preston's tutelage, Hilliard moved to Athens, Georgia to study law for nearly two more years in the office of Judge Augustin Smith Clayton.[15] Neither man wrote about their relationship, and Hilliard's decision to study under an extreme States' Rights advocate who had been elected Congress in 1831 as a Jacksonian Democrat is surprising. Hilliard neither supported Clayton's radical southern rights position nor shared his party affiliation. What perhaps drew Hilliard to Clayton was his prominence as a superior court judge with an intimate and well-documented knowledge of the law.[16] Exposure to Clayton's extreme States' Rights philosophy and his strong Jack-

---

[14] An 1812 graduate of South Carolina College with legal training at the University of Edinburgh, Scotland, Preston was a superior orator who at one time or another served as a member of the South Carolina House of Representatives, a United States Senator, and the President of South Carolina College. Preston, *Reminiscences of William C. Preston*; and for Preston's oratorical reputation, see LaBorde, *A History of the South Carolina College*, 289-290.

[15] See "Hon. Henry Washington Hilliard," *American Whig Review*, 610; and Lucian Lamar Knight, *A Standard History of Georgia and Georgians*, in 6 Vols. (Chicago: Lewis Publishing Company, 1917), 6: 3009-3010. Clayton was a distinguished lawyer who was selected by the Georgia state legislature in 1810 to compile the statutes of Georgia; was a member of the Georgia house of representatives from 1810-1812; elected a member of the state senate from 1826-1827; served as judge of the superior court from 1819-1825, and 1828-1831; and was elected as a Jacksonian Democrat to the Twenty-second and Twenty-third United States Congresses. See *Biographical Directory of the United States Congress*. See also, Knight, *Georgia and Georgians*, 6: 3009-3010.

[16] Augustin Smith Clayton, *A Compilation of the Laws of the State of Georgia, Passed by the Legislature Since the Political Year 1800, to the Year 1810, Inclusive* . . . (Augusta: Adams and Duyckinck, 1812).

sonian principles may have in fact simply reinforced Hilliard's quite different views.[17]

Hilliard was admitted to the Georgia Bar a few days after his twenty-first birthday and for a short time pursued a private law practice in Athens, Georgia.[18] It is curious that Hilliard did not choose the predictable course of returning to Columbia to practice where he had many connections and friends. His new and passionate involvement with the Methodist Church may explain why he stayed in Georgia, because while practicing law he also served as an itinerant minister.[19] Hilliard maintained a life-long affiliation with Methodism, and especially relied on his strong faith during times of stress. Hilliard attended the annual South Carolina Methodist Conference held at his hometown of Columbia, South Carolina, and on January 27, 1830, he was admitted to the Methodist ministry.[20] His work as both a preacher and an attorney soon gained him wide recognition in Georgia. It was, however, a difficult and often frustrating task to become a sole practitioner of law in Georgia and Alabama during the early nineteenth century, and the call

---

[17] In a period study of the Georgia Bar, Stephen Miller wrote that Clayton pressed "the doctrine of State sovereignty far ahead of any previous avowals by politicians . . . ." Stephen F. Miller, *The Bench and Bar of Georgia: Memoirs and Sketches* (Philadelphia: J.B. Lippincott and Company, 1858), 139.

[18] Athens was a town of approximately 600 white residents and 500 slaves. Augustus Longstreet Hull, *Annals of Athens, Georgia, 1801-1901* (Athens: Banner Job Office, 1906), 97.

[19] "Hon. Henry Washington Hilliard," *American Whig Review*, 610. During this period, Hilliard accepted the tenets of the Methodist Episcopal Church which exhibited "the strong resemblance of some of its usages to Puritan habits."

[20] Hilliard Records, Commission on Archives and History, Alabama-West Florida Conference, United Methodist Church, Huntingdon College Library.

of the Methodist Church became stronger than the appeal of Hilliard's new law practice.[21]

With the lure of self-advancement and political possibilities always tugging at him, Hilliard did not long confine his energies to the ministry. In 1830, he became editor of the *Columbus Enquirer*—the first of several newspapers with which he would be associated during his career.[22] The newspaper provided Hilliard with a vehicle for the expression of his opinions as well as providing a valuable experience that he would later use in editing two Alabama newspapers. At the same time, access to the press provided an obvious and common springboard for a political career.

Hilliard's growing reputation as a lawyer, scholar, preacher, editor, and orator was remarkable for a young man who had just reached the age of twenty-three. Recognizing Hilliard's impressive talents, in 1831 the newly established University of Alabama offered him the Chair in English Literature. The position afforded Hilliard the opportunity to teach constitutional law, rhetoric, elocution, and literature to the first class of the new institution, and to immerse himself in the subjects that had so deeply influenced his own thought and career.[23] As a teacher,

---

[21] For the challenges of establishing a law practice during this period, see Joseph G. Baldwin, *The Flush Times of Alabama and Mississippi. A Series of Sketches* (New York: D. Appleton and Company, 1854), 47-72, 223-250.

[22] George F. Mellen, "Henry Washington Hilliard and William Lowndes Yancey," *The Sewanee Review* 17 (1909): 33; and Lucian Lamar Knight, *Georgia's Landmarks, Memorials, and Legends* (Atlanta: Byrd Printing Company (for the author), 1913-1914), I: 818-819.

[23] See University of Alabama, *A Register of the Officers and Students of the University of Alabama, 1831-1901. Compiled by Thomas Waverly Palmer* (Tuscaloosa: The University, 1901), 23; Evans C. Johnson, "A Political Life of Henry W. Hilliard," (Thesis, University of Alabama, 1947), 2; and Golden, "The Political Speaking of Henry Washington Hilliard," 34.

Hilliard could use his oratorical and legal skills, as well as his extensive knowledge of literature. Even at this new institution, a university professor held a desirable and highly visible position that greatly appealed to the young Hilliard. Like many South Carolina College graduates, Hilliard migrated west where he became a prominent citizen on the cotton frontier of the Old Southwest.[24] With the appointment to the position at Alabama, Hilliard's somewhat erratic professional path had seemingly reached a logical destination, and he looked forward to a new career that promised to enlist his talents, offering him the respect and public platform for which he yearned.

Hilliard attempted to structure his life in the classical mold of ancient literary figures, such as Cicero and Demosthenes, whose oratory he so admired.[25] For Hilliard, their oratory seemed to be a means for exerting a certain mastery over their own times, and even achieving a degree of immortality.[26] With these examples in mind, Hilliard applied himself to various professions including law, the

---

[24] Hollis, *South Carolina College*, I: 42. Indeed, Anderson Crenshaw, the first graduate of South Carolina College, left his home state to pursue a legal career in Alabama as a state judge.

[25] Hilliard's interest in Demosthenes was likely stimulated by comparing his own goals and accomplishments to those of the great Athenian orator who, after practicing law for years, left his legal career to become a political orator in defense of Greek liberty. Demosthenes was a favorite subject of southern college literary societies. Many students during the early nineteenth century closely studied his life, speeches, and viewed him as the ideal of extemporaneous speaking. See E. Merton Coulter, *College Life in the Old South* (Athens: The University of Georgia Press, 1951 (1928)), 103-108.

[26] See William R. Smith, *Reminiscences of a Long Life; Historical, Political, Personal and Literary* (Washington, D.C.: William R. Smith, 1889), 214-215. Smith, one of Hilliard's first students, became a lawyer, author of prose and poetry, United States congressman, and president of the University of Alabama. See Thomas M. Owen, *History of Alabama and Dictionary of Alabama Biography* (Chicago: S.J. Clarke Publishing Company, 1921), IV: 1597-1598.

ministry, academia, and even international diplomacy that allowed him to occupy stages from which to pursue his soaring ambition.[27] Had he failed at any of these pursuits, he might have had to focus his efforts more narrowly, but success—at least in everything except teaching—encouraged him to pursue a wide range of occupations throughout his life.[28]

As Hilliard settled in to his new routine at the University of Alabama, he could not help but notice similarities to his experiences in South Carolina. The curriculum at the two institutions was similar and Hilliard was well acquainted with the course requirements and methods of instruction at the new university. In addition, literary societies were strongly encouraged as they had been at South Carolina College during Hilliard's tenure. Hilliard soon discovered another strong similarity between South Carolina College and his new school—a serious lack of discipline.[29] The sort

---

[27] Hilliard, in addition to his law practice, itinerant ministry, and faculty position at the University of Alabama, would be elected to a term as an Alabama state representative, appointed United States *chargé d'affaires* to Belgium, elected to three consecutive terms in the United States House of Representatives from the Montgomery, Alabama district, and later served as United States minister to Brazil.

[28] Hilliard was pleased with the academic profession in general and by all accounts was successful in his role as professor. William R. Smith wrote that he "seemed to take infinite delight in this occupation." However, the frontier nature of the university and sharp divisions among the faculty with respect to student discipline tainted his enjoyment of teaching to the point that prevented him from continuing in the occupation or ever returning to it. See Smith, *Reminiscences of a Long Life*, 221.

[29] Entries in the university's records of undisciplined behavior during the early years were common, and the lack of control within the student population became a serious problem at the school. The unrestrained nature of many of the students at Alabama likely reminded Hilliard of his days at South Carolina College where stories of the student rebellion of 1822, as well as an institutional memory of the persistent removal of the stairs to the Chapel in 1823 created humorous, if not dangerous, scenes of the entire faculty at times "walking the ladder" up

of misconduct that Hilliard had witnessed in the 1820s at Columbia was pervasive in the 1830s at Tuscaloosa. Alabama itself had only been a state for twelve years and the university reflected a decidedly frontier atmosphere, built appropriately enough on land that had once been part of a large cotton plantation.[30] Planters' sons and frontier folk made up the first classes at the university, and articulate, educated, and refined men such as Hilliard stood in sharp contrast to the general run of people eagerly clearing land, building houses, and obsessed with agricultural production.[31]

---

the six foot elevation. In 1822, one-third of the junior class was expelled from the college. LaBorde, *History of the South Carolina College,* 129-132, 140-143.

[30] See Smith, *Reminiscences of a Long Life,* 203; Matthew William Clinton, *Tuscaloosa, Alabama: Its Early Days, 1816-1865* (Tuscaloosa: The Zonata Club, 1958), 104-105. Six years before the University of Alabama opened its doors to the first class of students, the land that its buildings occupied in 1831 was a functioning cotton plantation owned by William M. Marr and worked by more than 100 slaves.

[31] Between 1810 and 1820, the population increased 1000 percent to 128,000. By 1830, it had reached 310,000 people. The new state of Alabama had experienced a population explosion following the Creek Indian land cessions gained by Andrew Jackson in 1814. The flood of migrants into Alabama was similar in scope to the 1848-1849 migrations to California. A good broad discussion of the Alabama patterns can be found in William Warren Rogers, Robert David Ward, Leah Rawls Atkins, and Wayne Flynt, *Alabama: The History of a Deep South State* (Tuscaloosa: The University of Alabama Press, 1994), 54-60. The diverse nature of the migrants is remarkable. Poor, marginal settlers sold everything and arrived with little supplies, small family farmers arrived ready to plant a cotton crop in the fertile new land, and well-supplied (frequently with slaves) young aspiring planters migrated to Alabama—the sons of wealthy Seaboard families who were not eligible to inherit their family's wealth. An additional perspective is offered in Joseph G. Baldwin, *The Flush Times of Alabama and Mississippi: A Series of Sketches* (New York: D. Appleton and Company, 1854) which describes, often in humorous terms, the vigorous period of development in Alabama and provides a contemporary look at the Alabama bench and bar. See also, Benjamin Buford Williams, *A*

His love of teaching and the adoration of his literary society students were not enough to satisfy the ambition of the young professor, and after several incidents involving a lack of discipline at the school Hilliard decided to leave the university to pursue a legal and political career in Montgomery, Alabama. Hilliard's choice of Montgomery was a good one, for it would replace Tuscaloosa as the capital of the state by the 1840s and it would bring him into the center of the state's political arena.[32]

Hilliard's interest in law and politics can be traced to, among other influences, his tutor and mentor, William Campbell Preston.[33] Preston had impressed upon Hilliard the advantages of the law for aspiring politicians. In an 1843 eulogy of Hugh S. Legaré, Preston repeated ideas that he had undoubtedly conveyed to young Hilliard years earlier:

> The profession of law in this country involves the cultivation of eloquence, and leads to political advancement and public honors. In this respect we nearly resemble the Roman Republic, and what is true of the whole country is more emphatically so of our own State. A preparation for the bar is supposed to be a preparation for public affairs; and it is the temper of the people to give their suffrages to those who come to it with a reputation of talents and

---

Literary History of Alabama: The Nineteenth Century (Rutherford: Fairleigh Dickinson University Press, 1979), 13.

[32] Tuscaloosa remained the intellectual center of the state; however, in 1846 the legislature selected Montgomery as the new site for the capital from a number of competing river towns.

[33] See Durham, "Henry Washington Hilliard," 21-22. Hilliard's strong interest in classical studies and oratory was developed through his experience at South Carolina College, and further reinforced by similar influences from his legal apprenticeship with William Campbell Preston.

learning.[34]

Hilliard's inclination to combine the interests of law and letters was far from unique in eighteenth and nineteenth-century America. The pairing of law and letters can be traced to the English Bar and its subsequent transference to eighteenth-century America.[35] In Alabama, as well as the South more generally, the idea of a close relationship between literary and legal training, eventually expanded to include the fine arts and the medical profession. Politics also had considerable influence over legal careers in towns and cities. Hilliard was a member of this rich literary and intellectual community. To most nineteenth-century Alabama authors, writing was more of an avocation pursued outside of the usual duties in the courtroom or legislature. One Alabama literary historian observes "the familiar pattern of lawyer-politician, and its variations of lawyer-editor, lawyer-historian, and editor-politician, is found in the biography of nearly every pre-Civil War writer in Alabama."[36] Within this extensive literary community of

---

[34] William C. Preston quoted in Ralph T. Eubanks, "An Historical and Rhetorical Study of the Speaking of William C. Preston." (Dissertation, University of Florida, 1957), 80. Preston not only served as an early tutor and influential figure in Hilliard's youth, but would by the 1840s facilitate Hilliard's entrance onto the national political stage. Many parallels can be drawn between Legaré's and Hilliard's political careers. It is likely through William Campbell Preston that the two were first introduced, and thus they traveled in similar circles. For Hugh Swinton Legaré, see Michael O'Brien, *A Character of Hugh Legaré* (Knoxville: University of Tennessee Press, 1985); and Linda Rhea, *Hugh Swinton Legaré, a Charleston Intellectual* (Chapel Hill: The University of North Carolina Press, 1934).

[35] See Wilfrid R. Prest, *The Rise of the Barristers: A Social History of the English Bar, 1590-1640* (Oxford: Oxford University Press, 1986), 184-208; and Robert A. Ferguson, *Law and Letters in American Culture* (Cambridge: Harvard University Press, 1984), 11-19.

[36] See Williams, *A Literary History of Alabama*, 27. Robert A. Ferguson, *Law and Letters in American Culture* (Cambridge: Harvard

lawyers, diplomats, legislators, academics, novelists, and even physicians, Hilliard felt at home for he was emblematic of the mixture of lawyer, statesman, novelist, and scholar, and moved from one circle to another with confidence and ease.

Despite a strong interest in religious activities and the law, by the mid 1830s Hilliard turned his attention more and more to politics. Montgomery by this time had become a community dominated by conservative planters who made the region a center of Whig politics.[37] It was therefore no accident that Hilliard chose Montgomery as the place to launch his political career. During contacts with the legislature in Tuscaloosa, he had become well acquainted with the complexity of Alabama's political landscape. He therefore deliberately moved to establish himself not only in the new capital's religious community, but also in the legal world that served as an entry point into

---

University Press, 1984), *passim*. One of the earliest observers of this connection between lawyer and the profession of letters was Thomas Jefferson, who regarded it as a natural tendency for an individual who was highly educated and had access to a certain amount of leisure time to gravitate toward letters. As early as 1803, lawyer, statesman, and author William Wirt observed, "Men of talents in this country . . . have been generally bred to the profession of law; and indeed, throughout the United States, I have met with few persons of exalted intellect, whose powers have been directed to any other pursuit. The bar, in America is the road to honour." See Richard Beale Davis, "The Early American Lawyer and the Profession of Letters," *Huntington Library Quarterly*, XII (1948-1949): 191-205. Political writing and orations satisfied literary standards, and it has been remarked of John C. Calhoun's political speeches that "it should be remembered that they come from an era in which deliberative oratory had not been divorced from relevance to political discourse, and political discourse had not been freed from the standards of literature. Clyde N. Wilson, *The Papers of John C. Calhoun*, volume XIV, 1837-1839 (Columbia: University of South Carolina Press, 1981), viii-ix.

[37] Flynt, *Montgomery: An Illustrated History*, 13; and the more comprehensive, Arthur Charles Cole, *The Whig Party in the South* (Washington: American Historical Association, 1913), 39-63.

politics. Although it was evident that through his under-standing and skill Hilliard would excel at the practice of law, the legal profession would always amount to a kind of second career for increasingly Hilliard focused his energy and aspirations on politics.

During the 1830s and 1840s Hilliard moved his way through the political and diplomatic maze serving as state representative; an appointment as United States chargé d'affaires to Belgium; and his eventual election as a Whig to the United States House of Representatives where he served from 1845 to 1851. It was Hilliard's election to Congress that excited him most, for he had realized a lifelong dream. As a member of the United States Congress he imagined himself poised to become the next great American orator, following in the footsteps of Clay, Webster, and Calhoun whom he had observed years earlier. Alarmed by the increasingly tense partisan and geograph-ical divisions, Hilliard took to Washington a public-spirited belief that sectional tensions could be subdued by reason and compromise. Since his earliest days at the University of Alabama, where thirteen years earlier he had delivered a speech on the character of the nation expressing the hope that violence in public life could be supplanted by reason, Hilliard deplored the rough and tumble, and especially the extremist aspects of American politics.[38] Armed with an elevated perception of what he could accomplish as a member of the Twenty-ninth Congress, Hilliard traveled to the nation's capital joining many newly elected members of the House, including southern representatives Jefferson Davis of Mississippi, and Robert Toombs of Georgia, as

---

[38]Henry W. Hilliard, *An Address Delivered Before the Erosophic Society, At its First Anniversary, May 26, 1832* (Tuscaloosa: Wiley, M'Guire and Henry, Printers, 1832), 4.

well as veterans Howell Cobb, William Lowndes Yancey, and Alexander Stephens.[39]

On arriving in Washington, Hilliard observed "a large number of able men, some of them already distinguished, and others destined to attain great places in the government of the country, and exert a powerful influence upon public affairs," and it is likely that he saw himself among the latter group.[40] Hilliard wasted little time engaging some of the toughest issues of the day such as the Oregon Territory, the Mexican War, and most significantly the debate on the constitutionality of American slavery, while consistently demonstrating his preference for national over sectional interests. Hilliard maintained a strong belief in political moderation; however, he also understood that he had an obligation to represent his constituents. Concerning the war with Mexico, Hilliard acknowledged the sectional dangers of territorial expansion, believing that the United States should avoid going to war simply to grab more territory. He also understood that slavery in the United States was a doomed institution and its demise was only a matter of time. Hilliard was certainly no radical abolitionist, but he strongly believed that the South was in a morally in-defensible position with respect to the issue of slavery. In an 1849 address to Congress, Hilliard responded to the ris-ing sentiment against the institution:

> There is a domestic institution in the South which in some sort insulates us from all mankind. The

---

[39] Ulrich Bonnell Phillips, ed., *The Correspondence of Robert Toombs, Alexander H. Stephens, and Howell Cobb* (Washington, 1913), II: 13-14.

[40] Henry W. Hilliard, *Politics and Pen Pictures at Home and Abroad* (New York: G.P. Putnam's Sons, 1892), 127. Hilliard describes "men of note in the House," offering (as he does throughout his rem-iniscences) not only physical descriptions of individuals, but also phrenology-type observations concerning their intellect.

civilized world is against us. I know it; I comprehend it; I feel it . . . Our moral condition at the South resembles the physical condition of Holland, where dikes, thrown up by the ingenuity of man, hardly protect the habitations of man against the incursions of the sea. If the South were in a commanding position, I should be willing to concede much; but because of her very weakness, I shall stand by her to the last.[41]

Hilliard's solution to the slavery question called on both sections to embrace a new commitment to the Missouri Compromise. Like many moderates in both parties, he believed that the most equitable solution would be to extend the 36-30 line to the Pacific Ocean. Hilliard had walked a very thin line between his belief in the destructive nature of sectional allegiances and the position in which the slavery issue and the Wilmot Proviso had placed him.

Despite many positive experiences in congress, Hilliard became disenchanted over his experience in Washington. During discussion of the Wilmot Proviso, Hilliard had warned, "This hall [Congress] should not be converted into an arena for hot controversy, by bringing for discussion here a subject which does not fairly come within the range of our deliberations, and which must shake, not only this Capitol, but this republic."[42] And in one of his most significant speeches on the issue of slavery, Hilliard warned his fellow congressmen, "the union of these states is in great peril."[43] Retreating to the church as he often did in times of

---

[41] Henry W. Hilliard, "Governments for the New Territories—The North and the South," *Speeches and Addresses* (New York: Harper and Brothers, 1855), 214-215.

[42] Hilliard, "The War with Mexico," *Speeches and Addresses*, 86-87.

[43] Hilliard, "Slavery and the Union, Remarks in the House of Representatives of the United States, December 12th, 1849," *Speeches and Addresses*, 226.

turmoil, Hilliard returned to the pulpit and the practice of law in Montgomery.[44] Hilliard found that the politics of slavery would continue to frustrate his classical ideal of peaceful debate and elevated statesmanship of which he had so often dreamed. In a speech to the Erosophic Society years earlier at the University of Alabama Hilliard had offered unknowingly what became a dark prophesy about his own public career:

> When, after the disastrous battle of Chaeronaea, Demosthenes was called upon to pronounce a funeral oration over the slain, he attempted it, and the occasion was surely a fine one; but it is remarked by the elegant historian of the period, "the complexion of the times no longer admitted those daring flights to which he had been accustomed to soar; and the powers of the orator seemed to have declined with the fortunes of his country . . . ."[45]

In great despair over the nation's political climate, Hilliard left Congress after serving his third term and aggressively pursued a diplomatic appointment using all of the political connections he could muster. He had enjoyed court life during his appointment as chargé d'affaires to Belgium, and lobbied for an appointment to France, Germany, or Russia.[46] As he became increasingly desperate over a diplomatic appointment, Hilliard wrote to President Millard Fillmore that if he did not receive an appointment

---

[44] For a detailed look at Hilliard's years in congress, see Durham, "Henry Washington Hilliard," 63-150.

[45] Hilliard, *An Address Delivered Before the Erosophic Society, At Its First Anniversary,* 8.

[46] Hilliard to Millard Fillmore, March 1849 through March 1853. Milliard Fillmore Papers, Buffalo and Erie County Historical Society, Buffalo, New York. Hereinafter, Millard Fillmore Papers.

soon, he would have to re-enter the practice of law.[47] The diplomatic appointment did not come, and Hilliard spent much of the prewar years practicing law in Montgomery and supporting moderate candidates for Congress.

Re-establishing a law practice in Montgomery proved bittersweet for Hilliard. After living in Washington for much of the time during his six years in congress, Hilliard enjoyed the opportunity to interact more intimately with family and local friends, and it is likely that he did not miss the acrimonious atmosphere of the House of Representatives. He did, however, miss the intellectual stimulation of his many northern friends and found little pleasure in his new law practice.[48] Hilliard had always envisioned himself as operating on a national or international stage and found Montgomery to be far too confining for a man of his ambitions.

In its second incarnation, Hilliard's law practice had changed significantly since his early career in the mid-1830s. From the time that he entered Congress until 1851, Hilliard had not actively practiced law except for appearing in old cases that reached the appellate courts, but he now developed a brisk and successful practice that many lawyers would envy. No longer was he a struggling attorney subsisting on Montgomery County cases, but instead he used his forensic skills and political reputation to greatly expand his legal horizons. Hilliard's practice during the 1850s included estate and land law, banking, and a

---

[47] Hilliard to Fillmore, March 20, 1851, Millard Fillmore Papers.

[48] For Hilliard's numerous letters and invitations to his northern friends, see Hilliard's correspondence with Nathan Appleton and Nathaniel Niles. For a sample of this type of correspondence, see Hilliard to Nathan Appleton, December 11, 1848, January 23, 1856, and July 11, 1856, Nathan Appleton Papers, Massachusetts Historical Society.

substantial number of criminal cases including two in which he represented slaves charged with murder.[49]

Although Hilliard was energized by the challenge of difficult cases, and certainly pleased by his success, he desperately missed the excitement of the political arena. When it came down to it, Hilliard could never be satisfied with just being a lawyer. He preached sermons, wrote literary pieces, and delivered speeches, but none of these activities could sate his appetite for a place on the political stage. Throughout the 1850s, Hilliard had been offered the presidency of several colleges. While flattered with such offers and an honorary Doctor of Laws degree, he showed no desire to retreat even further from the political stage into academia.[50]

By 1861, however, Hilliard's worst fears were realized as one southern state after another passed ordinances for secession in their state legislatures. Hilliard had lost considerable political influence in his hometown during the years following his departure from Congress. He became keenly aware of his political isolation as Jefferson Davis' inauguration as president approached. Hilliard had attempted to get a Methodist appointed as the spiritual leader of the occasion, but failed. As Basil Manly, who was appointed

---

[49] For Hilliard's appellate case record, see the *Alabama Reports of Cases Argued and Determined in the Supreme Court of Alabama*, for the years 1850-1860. Hilliard had defended at least two slaves who were charged with the murder or the attempted murder of white citizens (punishment of slaves was often significantly more severe for crimes against white persons). In the case of *Anthony v. The State*, Hilliard won a reversal for a slave who had attempted to poison his owner and the owner's wife. Although Anthony's conviction and death sentence were reversed, it is not known whether the case was retried. See 29 *Alabama Reports*, 27-30 (1856). For the widely cited case, *Bob v. The State*, see Durham, "Henry Washington Hilliard," 168-170; and 29 *Alabama Reports*, 20-27 (1856).

[50] Hilliard to David Lewis Dalton, December 29, 1858, Hilliard Papers, Alabama Department of Archives and History, Montgomery, Alabama.

chaplain for the event remarked, Hilliard "was against the Secession movement, as long as he could be" and had lost all consideration from the radicals.[51]

Until Abraham Lincoln called for an army to coerce the wayward states back into the Union following events at Fort Sumter, Hilliard had stoutly resisted secession. Yet Hilliard also favored a strict construction of the Constitution and believed that Lincoln had no power to address the crisis without the approval of Congress.[52] On Lincoln's decision, a disappointed Hilliard wrote "The crisis called for statesmanship of the highest order . . . not a rash and imperious act of usurped authority, such as might have been expected from the absolute ruler of a despotic state."[53] To Hilliard's way of thinking, Lincoln's call for troops had finally pushed staunch Unionists such as himself into the arms of the secessionists.

Although Hilliard had been snubbed by the Confederate administration, news of his conversion led Davis' Secretary of War, LeRoy P. Walker to call on Hilliard in May, 1861, to serve as commissioner to Tennessee.[54] The Davis administration saw an advantage to sending a moderate, pro-Union representative to convince reluctant Tennesseans to embrace secession as a necessity for self-preservation. Hilliard's success in Nashville once again set him to dreaming about a diplomatic post. Hilliard wrote to Vice-President Alexander Stephens several times asking him to recommend that Davis appoint him to the first available diplomatic post. Hilliard even suggested that, with Yancey due

---

[51] W. Stanley Hoole, "The Diary of Dr. Basil Manly, 1858-1867," *Alabama Review* 4 (1951): 147.

[52] Hilliard, *Politics and Pen Pictures*, 324.

[53] *Ibid.*

[54] Hilliard, *Politics and Pen Pictures*, 325-330. Clement A. Evans, ed., *Confederate Military History*, Vol. 8 (Atlanta: The Blue and Grey Press, 1899), 5-6. Also, for a brief treatment of Hilliard's mission to Tennessee, see Bryce Wray, "The Revolt of Tennessee From the Union in 1861," Unpublished Paper, East Texas State University, 1978.

to return from Europe following his resignation as Confederate diplomatic representative to England and France, he might replace him.[55] Otherwise, Hilliard specifically mentioned appointments to St. Petersburg or Madrid following diplomatic recognition of the Confederacy by those countries, which of course, never materialized.[56] Although Hilliard had served the fledgling Confederacy in Tennessee, he apparently received no serious consideration for a coveted diplomatic appointment.[57]

Hilliard's much-desired return to diplomatic service would ironically come at the end of Reconstruction as the result of the pairing of his strong Unionism and his short service to the Confederacy. Hilliard moved to Augusta, Georgia during the war and after having been overwhelmingly defeated in his bid for a congressional seat as a Republican candidate from Georgia during the 1876 congressional race, Hilliard would never again be tempted to run for public office. Out of 19,582 votes cast, he could garner but twenty-nine percent.[58] Significantly for Hilliard, however, Republican candidate Rutherford B. Hayes claimed the presidency in a fiercely disputed election and recognized the need to develop a new southern policy that might build Republican strength in the South, especially by

---

[55] Stanley Hoole, ed., "William L. Yancey's European Diary, March-June 1861," *Alabama Review* 25 (1972): 134-135. Many southerners were not surprised that Yancey's mission ended in failure as he had the reputation of being inherently un-diplomatic. Eric H. Walther, *The Fire-Eaters* (Baton Rouge: Louisiana State University Press, 1992), 79; and *William Lowndes Yancey and the Coming of the Civil War* (Chapel Hill: The University of North Carolina Press, 2006).

[56] Hilliard to Alexander Stephens, n.d., Alexander H. Stephens Papers, Emory University Library, Atlanta, Georgia.

[57] Hilliard briefly joined the war effort on behalf of the Confederacy but soon after resigned and spent the remaining war years in Georgia. Hilliard was a man of letters and oratory, not a man suited to field service. See Durham, "Henry Washington Hilliard," 184-189.

[58] Moore, ed., *Congressional Quarterly's Guide to U.S. Elections*, II: 918.

appealing to former Whigs. It is in fact likely that defeat in the 1876 congressional race spared Hilliard from significant frustration in a congress even more contentious than the one that he had grown to despise in 1851.

In fact, his pathetic showing in the election undoubtedly spurred Hilliard's determination to win through patronage what he could not win at the polls. For the sixty-nine-year-old Hilliard, this was perhaps the last chance for a political appointment. He joined the mass of office-seekers who always descended on Washington after a change of administration.[59] Hilliard spent an evening with good friend and former Whig congressman, Richard W. Thompson who had just been appointed Secretary of the Navy. Thompson reported that the president planned to offer Hilliard a diplomatic position. Hilliard hardly could have anticipated receiving such good news so quickly. Hilliard had been actively seeking any opportunity to secure a diplomatic appointment since his last session in Congress almost thirty years earlier. Thompson escorted Hilliard to the State Department where he introduced him to Secretary of State William M. Evarts who informed Hilliard that the president had approved him to succeed John C. Bancroft Davis as minister to Germany.[60] An elated Hilliard returned to Georgia and told his family the unbelievably good news of his pending appointment. However, Hilliard had barely had time for the initial excitement to wear off when he received a note from Evarts requesting his return to Washington at once. It seemed that Davis' departure from Germany had been delayed and it would be some time before the German position would be available. Secretary Evarts, however, noted that the mission in Brazil was available immediately. Speaking candidly, Evarts told Hilliard that he was aware of his hopes for a European post and that South America

---

[59] Hilliard, *Politics and Pen Pictures*, 356.
[60] *Ibid.*, 357.

might not be agreeable to him. Without delay Hilliard arranged to see the president to discuss the matter.[61]

To come so close to his dream of another diplomatic post and leave empty handed must have been almost unthinkable to Hilliard. Speaking to the president about the Brazil position, Hilliard respectfully asked, "Mr. President, ought I to accept it?"[62] While Hayes counseled Hilliard that he did not wish to speak for him, he confided that through the Brazil appointment, Hilliard could serve his country as well as his section. Hayes and Secretary of State Evarts were committed to much-needed improvements in the consular service, and one of the primary goals was to promote American trade abroad—especially in Latin America.[63] Hayes was eager to appoint southerners where it was possible—especially consular veterans—and Hilliard was a good fit for the Brazil post. A lifelong southerner and Confederate veteran, Hilliard was also a Republican who was on record as supporting the administration's policies.[64] Among other talents that Hilliard could take to Brazil, according to Hayes, he could be of invaluable assistance to the large numbers of southerners who had migrated to that country after the war.[65] Several thousand Americans had emigrated to Brazil along with thousands of other ex-

---

[61] *Ibid.*, 357-358.

[62] *Ibid.*, 358.

[63] In line with the president's policy of using appointments to pacify tensions in the South, Hilliard received the Brazil post and Cassius Goodloe of Kentucky, the Belgian mission. Kenneth E. Davidson, *The Presidency of Rutherford B. Hayes* (Westport: Greenwood Press, Inc., 1972), 197-199.

[64] Hayes rejected the idea of a strict policy to appoint only ruling party members, and Hilliard benefited from his overtures to the administration. Hayes, although rejecting strict patronage, believed that "those will be preferred who sympathize with the party in power." Leonard D. White, *The Republican Era: 1869-1901* (New York: The Macmillan Company, 1958), 122.

[65] Hilliard, *Politics and Pen Pictures*, 358.

patriates who had settled in Mexico and other Latin American countries.[66] Hayes hoped that Hilliard's Confederate credentials as well as his considerable powers of persuasion would convince many reluctant or struggling expatriates to return to their country. The president's argument was persuasive. Although Brazil was hardly his first choice, Hilliard's years of yearning for an appointment had taught him not to be greedy and he accepted the offer immediately. The president had deftly played to Hilliard's vanity as well as his desire to be of some assistance to fellow southerners in need. Hayes promptly made the appointment, and Hilliard returned to Georgia to prepare for his new assignment.[67]

After settling his family in residence in Europe, which was customary for diplomats working in parts of South America because of the seasonal health risks, Hilliard began the voyage to Brazil and reveled in the exotic adventure that he was undertaking.[68] As Hilliard entered Guanabara Bay at Rio de Janeiro, he was justifiably overwhelmed by what he saw before him.

> The scenery which rose to view was surpassingly
> beautiful; not only was the tropical verdure in

---

[66] Cyrus B. Dawsey and James M. Dawsey, editors, *The Confederados: Old South Immigrants in Brazil* (Tuscaloosa: The University of Alabama Press, 1995), xii, 3. Lawrence F. Hill, *Diplomatic Relations Between the United States and* Brazil (Durham: Duke University Press, 1932), 239; and Norman T. Strauss, "Brazil in the 1870s as Seen by American Diplomats," (Dissertation, New York University, 1971), 115.
[67] Hilliard, *Politics and Pen Pictures*, 358. Hilliard was formally appointed to the position of Envoy Extraordinary and Minister Plenipotentiary on July 31, 1877. He presented his credentials at the mission in Rio de Janeiro on October 23, 1877. Hilliard was commissioned during a recess of the Senate and was re-commissioned after confirmation by the Senate on February 7, 1878. See, United States Department of State, *United States Chiefs of Mission, 1778-1982*, 28.
[68] Durham, "Henry Washington Hilliard," 212-213.

perfection, but the whole aspect of the coast far transcended anything in sublimity that I had seen in any country. The morning was bright; not a cloud shut out of view any point of the unrivalled picture that opened before us. There was a blended majesty and beauty—an expanding stretch of water, a range of mountains towering to great heights, on some sides precipitous and bare, and on others robed in the green verdure of the tropics. The Bay of Rio de Janeiro is the most beautiful in the world.[69]

The sights were perhaps especially beautiful to an American, particularly to a southern escapee whose ambitions might at last be fulfilled. Before Hilliard disembarked at Rio de Janeiro, a number of Americans came on board his ship to offer him a celebratory welcome and transportation to his new home. He was met with considerable hospitality and after a small reception in his honor, he began to settle in at his apartments at the *Hotel dos Estrangeiros*. On the walls in the main salon were portraits of George Washington, King Leopold I of Belgium, and Queen Victoria. Comforted by the familiarity of the notable figures, Hilliard later commented, "The pictures seemed to welcome me."[70]

Unpacking his books, papers, and other belongings, Henry W. Hilliard was pleased as he familiarized himself with his new surroundings at the American legation in Rio de Janeiro. Likely exceeding his expectations, the building and grounds of the legation were palatial. The United States legation consisted of a large Mediterranean-style building with sweeping verandas, palace-sized rooms, extensive formally-landscaped gardens, and was situated among large imperial palms and breadfruit trees on the slopes of a

---

[69]Hilliard, *Politics and Pen Pictures*, 362.
[70] *Ibid.*, 363.

forested mountainside.[71] The tropical setting was, however, not as idyllic as it seemed. The same climate that created the beauty that impressed Hilliard throughout his tenure in Brazil also created unexpected challenges for the diplomat. The heat, humidity, and insects in Rio de Janeiro made it necessary for Hilliard's predecessors to store critical records of the legation in metal cases at the summer retreat at Petrópolis where the imperial court and diplomatic corps resided from November through April.[72] It did not take Hilliard long, however, to adjust to the rhythms of his new assignment, and he anticipated his role as the ranking representative of the United States to Brazil.

The colony of Brazil thrived throughout the sixteenth, seventeenth, and eighteenth centuries, fueled primarily from sugar production utilizing African slave labor until the early nineteenth century. In 1808 under the threat of conquest by Napoleon's troops, the entire Portuguese court had sailed to Brazil and transferred the seat of the Portuguese empire to Rio de Janeiro.[73] With significant assistance from Great Britain, regent Dom João, his family,

---

[71] The American legation/embassy during the nineteenth century is now the *Escola Alemã* at *São Clemente*. The site is located near the Imperial Palace and backs up to the slopes of *Corcovado* mountain. For verification of the site of the United States Embassy prior to the Consulate's present location, Pamela Howard-Reguindin, Field Director, Library of Congress Office, Rio de Janeiro to author, December 6, 2004.

[72] The diplomatic corps and imperial court spent summers in the mountain retreat to protect against the heat and disease in Rio de Janeiro. Hilliard to Secretary of State William Maxwell Evarts, October 19, 1877. For correspondence from the Brazil legation to the State Department during Hilliard's tenure, see *Despatches from United States Ministers to Brazil*, United States Department of State, M121, roll 44 (May 25, 1875-August 28, 1877), roll 45 (October 19, 1877-August 30, 1879), and roll 46 (September 1, 1879-September 27, 1881), hereinafter *Despatches*.

[73] João Pandiá Calogeras, *A History of Brazil* (Chapel Hill: The University of North Carolina Press, 1939), 55-56.

and fifteen thousand members of the Portuguese court had engaged in a remarkable political and cultural transference to the colonial capital of Rio de Janeiro.[74] Profiting from a commercial and cultural expansion that was no longer limited by its colonial status, Brazil experienced a new era of banking, commerce, and inter-national trade—especially with its close friend Great Britain—that far surpassed its former standing.[75]

Not surprisingly, the prolonged relocation of the throne in Rio de Janeiro, as well as the elevation of Brazil to the status of kingdom in 1815, caused significant problems for Dom João in Lisbon.[76] On April 26, 1821 Dom João sailed for Lisbon, taking most of the specie in the Bank of Brazil, all of the jewels that he could readily gather, and approximately three thousand members of the Portuguese court. Leaving his young son Dom Pedro in Brazil as regent, he strongly advised the young royal to seize the Brazilian crown for himself as soon as possible, or risk losing it to either political opportunists or republican movements.[77] Dom João VI had left his twenty-four year old son with the difficult task of establishing himself as monarch in

---

[74] Dom João served as regent of the empire on behalf of his mother, Dona Maria I who was insane, and formed what became the only successful non-indigenous establishment of an American monarchy. Calogeras, *A History of Brazil*, 50. Not only did Dom João move his court, but he also shipped a significant amount of Portugal's national culture. To prevent the treasures from being sacked by Napoleon, the crown shipped irreplaceable materials including books, manuscripts, engravings, maps, incunabula, artwork and specie to Brazil. Paulo Herkenhoff, *Biblioteca Nacional: A História de uma Coleção* (Rio de Janeiro: Salamandra Consultoria Editorial, 1996), 5-6.

[75] C.H. Haring, *Empire in Brazil: A New World Experiment with Democracy* (Cambridge: Harvard University Press, 1958), 6-7.

[76] In 1816, Maria I died and Dom João VI became King of the United Kingdom of Portugal, Brazil and the Algarve. Haring, *Empire in Brazil*, 10.

[77] Calogeras, *A History of Brazil*, 68-71; and Haring, *Empire in Brazil*, 13.

45

the midst of a continent seething with independence movements. Dom Pedro's many personal shortcomings magnified the difficulty of his situation. It was, however, when the young royal was ordered to return to Lisbon to complete his political education, that he refused and declared both his and Brazil's independence from Portugal.[78]

Dom Pedro I's troubled reign as Emperor of Brazil lasted only nine years. Following a number of poor decisions and growing discontent with his rule—including widespread disapproval of his concubine—the emperor's ability to govern decreased dramatically during the late 1820s. Dom Pedro I was forced to abdicate the throne in 1831 in favor of his five-year-old son, Pedro de Alcântara. Following his departure for Europe, the French *chargé d'affaires* wrote that the emperor "knew better how to abdicate than to reign."[79]

---

[78] Dom Pedro received almost no formal education. His informal education came from palace servants and devotees who catered to his whims, resulting in a poorly-behaved young man who in his early years became known more for his practical jokes than his potential for leadership. Calogeras, *A History of Brazil*, 72-73. On September 7, 1822, Dom Pedro drew his sword in indignation of the liberals in Portugal who had terrorized his father, and proclaimed "The hour has come! Independence or death! We have separated from Portugal! Dom Pedro's declaration near the small stream, Ipiranga, is known as the "Cry of Ipiranga" and marks Brazilian independence from Portugal. Haring, *Empire in Brazil*, 16-17. Brazil declared its independence from Portugal in 1822; however, it did not suffer the same violence and bloodshed that its neighbors did in their transition from Spanish colonies to independent republics. Between 1806 and 1826, Spanish America broke apart into a series of independent republics through a cycle of bloody wars. For Spanish American wars of independence, see John Lynch, *The Spanish American Revolutions, 1808-1826* (New York: W.W. Norton and Company, 1973), 1-3, *passim*.

[79] Calogeras, *A History of Brazil*, 107-118. By the end of the decade, he was accused of governing contrary to his own constitution, and open revolt spilled into the streets of Rio de Janeiro. Dom Pedro I arranged for his most competent former minister José Bonifácio de Andrada e Silva to serve as the child's tutor and mentor. Roderick J. Barman,

46

Pedro de Alcântara, in sharp contrast to his father, was groomed for the throne and developed a keen grasp of both domestic and international issues prior to his coronation. The young man was very well educated, reared as an enlightened liberal, and assumed the throne in 1841 at the age of fifteen when he was crowned "Dom Pedro II, Constitutional Emperor of Brazil."[80] Although he was a competent and intellectual leader who was responsible for many positive accomplishments during his reign, by 1877 Dom Pedro II faced an increasing number of serious challenges to his authority.

For his part as Envoy Extraordinary and Minister Plenipotentiary, Hilliard found himself not only living and working in a tropical environment, but more importantly representing the United States at a most difficult time in Brazilian history.[81] Hilliard had read about Brazil and was familiar with the serious issues that confronted the emperor. One of the most explosive was African slavery, which had troubled Dom Pedro II throughout most of his reign. By 1877 the pressure on Brazil to deal with the question was mounting, and following the end of slavery in the United States, only Cuba and Brazil still clung to the institution.[82] Also of immediate concern to both the Brazilians and Hilliard was the recent war with Paraguay. The

Citizen Emperor: Pedro II and the Making of Brazil, 1825-91 (Stanford: Stanford University Press, 1999), 33. For a brief treatment of Dom Pedro I's abdication, see Haring, *Empire in Brazil*, 41-43.

[80] Lilia Moritz Schwarcz, *The Emperor's Beard: Dom Pedro II and the Tropical Monarchy of Brazil* (New York: Hill and Wang, 2004), 51-57.

[81] Hilliard announced his arrival to Brazil's Foreign Minister Diogo Velho Cavalcanti de Albuquerque on October 18, 1877, Correspondence Book # 1, *Estados Unidos Notas* 1877-1880, *Arquivo do Museu Histórico e Diplomático, Palácio Itamaraty*, Rio de Janeiro, Brazil. Hereinafter, *Arquivo Itamaraty*.

[82] Seymour Drescher and Stanley L. Engerman, editors, *A Historical Guide to World Slavery* (New York: Oxford University Press, 1998), 100.

War of the Triple Alliance (1864-1870) had pitted Brazil, Argentina, and Uruguay against the aggressor Paraguay in a long and bloody conflict. Paraguay was left prostrate by the war, and Brazil had suffered heavy losses. The war left Brazil more dependent than ever on trade with Great Britain and also wary of the designs of a potentially aggressive Argentina.[83] Hilliard found a favorable environment for improving relations and promoting increased trade with Brazil.

Friendly relations between the United States and Brazil dated back to the late eighteenth century when both countries had a common interest in avoiding European monarchical ties. Brazilians greatly admired the American Revolution and the ideology that inspired it. The country's leaders were not only familiar with translations of the American Constitution, but had also closely read the Federalist Papers and other Revolutionary-era documents.[84] The United States in turn, shared Brazil's interest in avoiding entanglements with European nations. In 1828 the two nations signed the mutually beneficial "Treaty of Peace, Friendship, Commerce, and Navigation."[85] During the 1860s, indifference and neglect under an inept corps of American diplomats strained relations between the two countries. By the 1870s, however, the United States began to appreciate the value of good relations with Brazil and the potential benefits to trade, social, and political concerns that would result from improved ties.[86]

---

[83] Schwarcz, *The Emperor's Beard*, 232-248.

[84] Joseph Smith, *History of Brazil, 1500-2000: Politics, Economy, Society, Diplomacy*, (London: Pearson Education, 2002), 17-19.

[85] Norman T. Strauss, "Brazil in the 1870s As Seen by American Diplomats," (Ph.D. dissertation, New York University, 1971), 1; 8 *United States Statutes*, Treaty Series, 34.

[86] Relations with Brazil reached a low point during the 1860s as a result of the behavior of, among others, Minister to Brazil, James Watson Webb. Unsuited to be a diplomat, Webb did not study Brazil's laws, treaties, customs, or language in preparation for his post, and openly

Hilliard clearly believed that his work extended far beyond the daily routine of a diplomatic mission. He must protect the honor and political interests of his country, and more importantly advance its commercial interests.[87] Hilliard traveled to Brazil with an enthusiasm and focus that he had not exhibited during his tenure as *chargé d'affaires* to Belgium, and seemed intent on distinguishing himself in his new post. Learning to read Portuguese in addition to familiarizing himself with Brazilian law, Hilliard was well prepared for his office. Even though Brazil had not been Hilliard's first choice for an appointment, he applied himself in a way that had not been evident since his first few months in Congress more than thirty-two years before.[88]

---

announced upon arriving in Rio de Janeiro that he could not read or speak the language and had no intention of learning. Webb had considered the post beneath him and selected a list of 150 novels to pass his time in Brazil. Webb insulted, and for a time severed, diplomatic relations with Brazil over a dispute concerning a Massachusetts whaler, *Canada* and another ship, *Caroline*. As a result, the United States' image in Brazil suffered for more than a decade. Strauss, "Brazil in the 1870s As Seen by American Diplomats," 2, 3-18.

[87] Henry W. Hilliard, "An Address to His Majesty Dom Pedro II, Constitutional Emperor and Perpetual Defender of Brazil by Henry W. Hilliard, Envoy Extraordinary and Minister Plenipotentiary of the United States of America," October 23, 1877, leaf 2-6. *Arquivo Itamaraty*. Also, Strauss, "Brazil in the 1870s As Seen by American Diplomats," 19.

[88] Even as his old colleagues congratulated him on his appointment to the Brazil post, Hilliard was reminded that it was not his first choice. Friend and fellow Georgian, Senator Benjamin H. Hill wrote to Hilliard, "I was sincerely rejoiced when I saw the notice of your appointment as Minister to Brazil. I had hoped it would have been to a still more important court." Hilliard seems to have been unshaken by the less important court because he took his responsibilities quite seriously. Benjamin H. Hill to Hilliard, August 15, 1877, *Despatches*. Hilliard to Secretary of State Evarts, October 1, 1878, *Papers Relating to the Foreign Relations of the United States . . . December 1, 1879* (Washington: Government Printing Office, 1879), 129. Hilliard demonstrated an ability to read Portuguese law by October 1878—and perhaps possessed a good reading ability in the language even earlier.

On October 18, 1877, Hilliard announced his official arrival as the replacement of James R. Partridge to Foreign Minister Diogo Velho C. de Albuquerque, as well as his request for an audience with the emperor in order formally to present himself and to deliver a letter from President Hayes.[89] Albuquerque promptly made the arrangements and Hilliard addressed the emperor in a formal ceremony at the royal palace at São Cristóvão on October 23, 1877.

At this first meeting, the two men exchanged prepared speeches. Hilliard wasted no time in engaging the interest of the emperor in one of his primary goals as minister to Brazil—improved trade between Brazil and the United States. Hilliard took the opportunity to congratulate the emperor on his recent trip to the United States, and complimented the "magnificent display . . . of the products and industry of Brazil at the International Exhibition." He assured the emperor that the exhibition "has increased our desire to strengthen the commercial relations between the two countries, and we hope to soon witness an improvement in the means for accomplishment of that object."[90] Hilliard emphasized to the emperor that although separate

---

[89] Hilliard to Diogo Velho C. de Albuquerque, October 18, 1877, Correspondence, *Arquivo Itamaraty.*

[90] Hilliard address to Dom Pedro II, October 23, 1877, Correspondence, *Arquivo Itamaraty.* The means to which Hilliard refers was the proposal of a direct steamship line between the United States and Brazil. Dom Pedro II traveled to the United States in May 1876 to visit the Universal Exhibition in Philadelphia. His visit received significant attention, in part because it was the first visit to the United States by a monarch. During his visit, Dom Pedro II was inspired by the exhibition as well as America's centennial celebrations. Dom Pedro II along side of President Ulysses S. Grant opened the Philadelphia Universal Exhibition and the emperor met, among others, Thomas Edison and Alexander Graham Bell. In New York, the emperor met with naturalist Louis Agassiz and Henry Wadsworth Longfellow, leaving North America with an elevated opinion of the United States and the need for improved relations with Brazil. Schwarcz, *The Emperor's Beard,* 275-277.

countries, Brazil and the United States were both "American" and stressed the opportunities for the two nations to strengthen their friendship.[91]

Hilliard had felt at ease with the emperor almost immediately despite the formality of the palace at São Cristóvão. After delivering his speech to the emperor—who stood during his presentation—Hilliard and Dom Pedro II enjoyed a more relaxed conversation. Speaking in English, the men discussed a number of topics and soon realized that they shared many interests. The emperor congratulated Hilliard on his many accomplishments, particularly his work with the Smithsonian Institution, and Hilliard spoke at length about his love for classical literature. The men closed the conversation with a general discussion of the racial situation in post-war Georgia.

During his tenure in Brazil, Hilliard developed a friendship with Dom Pedro II outside of their official relations. Hilliard had arrived in Brazil in October, 1877, when the imperial family and most of the diplomatic corps prepared to travel, first to their summer quarters in Tijuca, and then to the summer palace high in the mountains at Petrópolis to escape the heat and disease in Rio de Janeiro.[92] At Petrópolis, Hilliard began cultivating his friendship with the emperor. The less formal mountain surroundings offered a more conducive environment for diplomats to socialize with the royal family. Hilliard and the emperor frequently enjoyed walks together, and the two

---

[91] Hilliard address to Dom Pedro II, October 23, 1877, Correspondence, *Arquivo Itamaraty.*

[92] Because of the threat of disease in Rio de Janeiro, the imperial court resided in Petrópolis, a mountain city about sixty-six kilometers from Rio de Janeiro, generally from November to April of each year. Hilliard to Evarts, October 19, 1877. *Despatches.*

men developed a friendship based on their numerous and mutual academic and literary interests.[93]

Dom Pedro II regularly took long daily walks in the morning and afternoon to relieve symptoms from his diabetes.[94] Taking advantage of the opportunity, Hilliard often joined the emperor on these walks and conversed with him on a quite personal level. It became significantly easier for Hilliard to establish a close and friendly relationship with the emperor than it had been for any of his diplomatic predecessors, and Hilliard used this access to address policy issues that he considered most important. In addition to their intellectual interests, the two men frequently discussed issues of current concern to their respective countries. Dom Pedro II and Hilliard discussed topics such as the emperor's controversial advocacy of the direct election of representatives, and the need for increased economic interaction between Brazil and the United States. And their conversations frequently turned to the sensitive issue of Brazilian slavery. Dom Pedro II was a liberal leader who was sympathetic to abolition, but his political survival required a cautious approach to the powerful and conservative planter class. Through his access to the emperor, Hilliard did much to improve the confidence and respect that Dom Pedro II felt for the American people, but

---

[93] Hilliard, *Politics and Pen Pictures*, 369, 380-381. Dom Pedro II was, above all, interested in the intellectual life. His interests included natural science, languages, art, and literature. Dom Pedro II frequently confessed that he would rather be a teacher than emperor, writing in his diary, "If I weren't emperor of Brazil, I would like to be a schoolmaster." Schwarcz, *The Emperor's Beard*, 113-114, 273.

[94] By 1877, the emperor had been suffering from type II diabetes for some time. His personal physician, Dr. Cláudio Velho da Mota Maia diagnosed Dom Pedro II in the late 1870s and among other measures, recommended that the emperor take long walks twice every day. See, Barman, *Citizen Emperor*, 300-301.

that impression represented only part of what Hilliard hoped to accomplish during his tenure in Brazil.[95]

Hilliard's efforts promoting trade between the two countries was a priority for him and his accomplishments did not go unnoticed by the Brazilian press. A liberal publication, *O Cruzeiro*, noted on October 22, 1878, that the establishment of a regular passenger and cargo line between the United States and Brazil that Hilliard had helped broker had immediately raised hopes for improved trade between the countries.[96]

In addition to trade concerns, Hilliard successfully juggled a number of important issues in his official capacity as minister. One of Hilliard's primary concerns was that of the thousands of southerners who had fled to Brazil during and shortly after the American Civil War. One of the reasons that President Rutherford B. Hayes had selected Hilliard for the Brazil post was his belief that the former southern congressman and Confederate soldier could persuade hundreds of American citizens who were suffering in Brazil to return home.[97] Following the Civil War, as many as ten thousand southerners fled the United States for various countries in Latin America in the hope of establishing a new life. In the unprecedented exodus, three or four thousand expatriates established several settlements in Brazil.[98]

Shortly after the war, two publications, Ballard S. Dunn's *Brazil, the Home for Southerners*, and James McFadden Gaston's *Hunting a Home in Brazil*, prompted

---

[95] Strauss, "Brazil in the 1870s As Seen by American Diplomats," 245-256; Hilliard, *Politics and Pen Pictures*, 365-370.

[96] *O Cruzeiro*, Rio de Janeiro, October 22, 1878. *Biblioteca Nacional*. For Hilliard's work with Brazilian trade and treaties, see Durham, "Henry Washington Hilliard," 225-229.

[97] Durham, "Henry Washington Hilliard," 213.

[98] Hill, *Diplomatic Relations Between the United States and Brazil*, 239.

many families to consider migrating south. Interested individuals included doctors, lawyers, planters, merchants, ministers, and outlaws, all hoping to find a new life in a country that not coincidentally still supported the institution of slavery. Dreams of a new cotton empire in Brazil induced migrants to liquidate their assets and settle in one of a number of locations from the southern province of Rio Grande to the Amazonian province of Pará farther to the north.[99]

The government of Brazil also tried to attract disgruntled southerners, often offering to pay for their passage and tempting them with inducements of heavily discounted lands in the remote settlements. Brazil had suffered from a serious labor shortage that worsened during the 1860s and 1870s, and American emigrants to Brazil were promised a number of inducements by Brazilian agents to attract migration. Land was offered to settlers for as little as twenty-two cents per acre including surveying and was arranged in large colonies that averaged 500,000 acres.[100] Diarist and expatriate American Julia L. Keyes described how the system of inducements and subsidies worked:

> Our Steamer was chartered by the Brazilian
> Government to carry Southern Emigrants to the
> Empire. She was a steam-propeller of 1300 tons,
> [and] was built three years before, for the
> transportation of Federal troops. The charter cost
> $40,000 in specie. The price for each emigrant
> being $60 in gold, to be paid, by each at the
> expiration of four years in biennial installments.[101]

---

[99] *Ibid.*, 243.

[100] *Ibid.*, 241. Land was priced from twenty-two to forty-two cents per acre including the cost of the survey.

[101] Julia L. Keyes, "Our Life, in Brazil," *Alabama Historical Quarterly* 28 (1966): 133. Keyes offered a quite detailed description of her journey with family and friends from Montgomery, Alabama, to a

While many emigrants successfully relocated, most were far less fortunate.[102] Brazil allowed each small colony to maintain an element of self-government that satisfied the settlers' desire for independence. Yet the Brazilian government failed to honor many of the promises made to the emigrants, in part because of the costs of the war with Paraguay.[103]

---

settlement near Linhares, Brazil, where the Gunter Colony had settled. Her account is a romanticized version of a short and eventually aborted settlement, ironically offering a derogatory view of mostly accommodating local populations. Keyes' journal offers detailed perceptions of her experience as an American expatriate in Brazil. Antebellum Alabama was a small world indeed. Hilliard saw many familiar faces among the expatriates in Brazil. Wade Keyes, who was a Montgomery, Alabama chancery judge before whom Hilliard had tried several cases, had two brothers among the emigrants—also whom Hilliard knew. George Keyes served as register in chancery and was associate editor of the Montgomery *Advertiser*. John Washington Keyes and his family were among the migrants who moved to Brazil with the Gunter Colony from Montgomery. John Keyes, at the request of Dom Pedro II, located in Rio de Janeiro and became dentist to the royal family. The Gunter Colony, which migrated to Brazil in 1867, was led by Wade Keyes' former law partner, Charles Grandison Gunter against whom Hilliard had practiced law. See, David I. Durham and Paul Pruitt, *Wade Keyes' Introductory Lecture to the Montgomery Law School: Legal Education in Mid-Nineteenth Century Alabama* (Tuscaloosa: University of Alabama School of Law, 2001), 6-7, note 18.

[102] Not surprisingly, William Lowndes Yancey's sons, Dalton and Benjamin, left the United States and relocated in Brazil with a colony that today is known as Americana, located near São Paulo. The Yancey name still survives there today. See, Eric Walther, *The Fire-Eaters* (Baton Rouge: Louisiana State University Press, 1992), 81.

[103] Keyes, "Our Life in Brazil," 150. Keyes reported from the Gunter settlement near Linhares that promises for transportation to the colonists by the emperor were not upheld because of the war with Paraguay. Brazil's war effort took precedent over broken promises and suffering Americans, and most of the infrastructure guarantees never materialized because Brazil simply did not have the resources available. Strauss, "Brazil in the 1870s As Seen by American Diplomats," 141.

Many Americans traveled to Brazil expecting to establish successful cotton plantations based on cheap land and African slave labor. Unfortunately for the emigrants, the new cotton kingdom never materialized. The combination of a severe drought that lasted almost two years, smallpox epidemics, and the cost of transporting bulky cotton over long distances kept production low. Many emigrant farmers adapted to the situation by shifting to the cultivation of beans, corn and sugar cane, and others tried their hand at raising cattle.[104] To add to their difficulty, an unusually high incidence of disease combined with drought challenged even the most stalwart settlers and hundreds found themselves destitute without the resources to stay in Brazil or return to the United States.[105]

The suffering of Americans in Brazil had been a problem long before Hilliard arrived at his post. As early as 1870, American minister Henry T. Blow acknowledged rumors of destitute Americans in the Pará region, although he dismissed the accounts as unofficial. "The principle American colony remaining in Brazil is engaged in the culture of cotton, and claims to be doing well, though most

---

[104] Lawrence F. Hill, "Confederate Exiles to Brazil," *Hispanic American Historical Review* 7 (1927): 206. During the 1870s drought and disease devastated the Brazilian interior provinces. In the hardest hit areas such as Ceará, corpses and carrion were converted into food by starving Brazilian residents. *New York Times*, December 27, 1878.

[105] Even under the best circumstances the climate could be brutal to foreigners not accustomed to it. Secretary of the American Legation, William Edwards' health forced him to resign from his post on March 12, 1878. Edwards had been in the country approximately six months when he experienced "a serious decline in health" that led to his resignation. He reported to Secretary of State Evarts that he left his post because "my health having broken down under the severe strain of this climate." William Edwards to Evarts, March 12, 1878, *Despatches*. Hilliard remarked on the harsh climate as he took inventory of the American ministry's library, noting that the thirty-volume set of the *Congressional Debates* was listed as "useless—destroyed by climate and insects." *Despatches*, front matter, roll 44.

of the members are dissatisfied, living frugally, and will doubtless return to their old homes as soon as their means will permit."[106] By the next year, American diplomat James R. Partridge reported the use of American military ships to transport repentant migrants without means back to the United States.[107] By 1872, Partridge acknowledged that these expatriates should perhaps be left to deal with their own troubles; however, there were women and children who had lost everything. They had no employment or means to return to the United States and, according to Partridge, deserved the government's assistance.[108]

By the time Hayes had appointed Hilliard to the Brazilian post, the official attitude toward stranded southerners had changed significantly. Hayes appeared determined to put wartime passions in the past and focus on humanitarian questions. Many heads of households had died from disease or starvation and there were shocking reports in the newspapers of destitute American women and children begging and living on the streets of Rio de Janeiro, often sick and with little clothing.[109] Faring even worse, some women and children were starving in the countryside on otherwise abandoned plantation sites.

---

[106] Henry T. Blow to Hamilton Fish, November 5, 1870. *Foreign Relations of the United States* (1871): 43.

[107] Partridge observed, "In the province of San[*sic*] Paulo, where I understand there are still between three and four hundred in all, very many of whom are exceedingly anxious to avail themselves of the generosity of our Government, which they are now glad to call their Government also, to return to the home they left." James R. Partridge to Hamilton Fish, September 8, 1871. *Foreign Relations of the United States* (1871): 64.

[108] James R. Partridge to Hamilton Fish, January 22, 1872. *Foreign Relations of the United States* (1872): 90.

[109] Strauss, "Brazil in the 1870s As Seen by American Diplomats," 123. The *New York Times* also reported Americans sleeping in the streets of Pará in 1879. February 23, 1879.

Several groups attempted to assist needy Americans. Wealthy American businessmen in Brazil donated passage money or found jobs for the sufferers, politicians in the United States often sent funds to transport former constituents, and the Brazilian government arranged temporary housing and jobs. The American Benevolent Society in Rio de Janeiro was organized for the rescue of women and children and worked closely with Hilliard. Several diplomats, including Hilliard, donated money to assist with some of the worst cases.[110] In his official capacity Hilliard could accomplish more for his fellow southerners by organizing transportation home. Working with Secretary of State Evarts and President Hayes, Hilliard coordinated the use of navy vessels to transport those without means to the United States. In addition, he arranged greatly reduced or free passage on the *City of Rio de Janeiro* for expatriate women and children who, for reasons of health or scheduling, could not be transported back to America by navy ship.[111]

Prior to his appointment to Brazil, Hilliard had earned a reputation for devoting most of his attention to larger issues and slighting more mundane matters. Now he paid a great deal of attention to serving the needs of Americans in Brazil.[112] In cases involving American claims against Brazil, Hilliard was able to employ not only his skills as a seasoned diplomat, but also those of an experienced lawyer.

---

[110] Strauss, "Brazil in the 1870s As Seen by American Diplomats," 118, 136. Blow, Partridge, and Hilliard donated personal funds for some of the most desperate cases.

[111] *New York Times*, February 23, 1879.

[112] For examples of Hilliard's daily correspondence, see representative letters such as the February 24, 1880 letter concerning the death of an ordinary American citizen, and the July 28, 1879 letter covering the forwarding of general correspondence between the state department and the Brazilian secretary of agriculture. Correspondence, *Arquivo Itamaraty*.

Performing official duties provided Hilliard with some satisfaction, but the issue of Brazilian slavery offered him a unique opportunity to rid himself of various personal demons. In fact, by November 1880, Hilliard had become so involved in the issue that it threatened his remaining tenure as minister. Brazil had long been a slaveholding society and during the seventeenth century the demand for African labor increased dramatically as the result of the tremendous growth in the production of sugar. A combination of a large sugar market with its insatiable labor demands and high mortality rates that prevented the establishment of a self-sustaining slave population helped the Brazilian market account for some thirty-eight percent of the total world market in slaves from 1500 to 1870.[113]

Although in many respects Dom Pedro II was an enlightened leader, the slavery issue tested his liberalism and potentially threatened his control of the country. Brazil's influential conservative planters represented a powerful political force whose sugar, coffee, and cotton fortunes rested on a reliable labor supply.[114] However strongly the emperor felt about the injustice of slavery, the conservatives held significant power and Dom Pedro II had been weakened by the Paraguayan War, making it necessary for him to tread lightly in any discussion of sudden and universal emancipation.[115] Dom Pedro II knew that he would have to address the country's labor question to satisfy the conservative opposition. Members of the liberal party agreed that the best approach to the abolition of

---

[113] Natural increases in the North American slave population had made it unnecessary to import slaves to maintain a captive work force. Brazil's thirty-eight percent compares to six percent for North America and represents the need to constantly re-supply the slave population. Robert William Fogel and Stanley L. Engerman, *Time on the Cross: The Economics of American Negro Slavery* (New York: W.W. Norton and Company, 1989 (1974)), 14.

[114] Strauss, "Brazil in the 1870s As Seen by American Diplomats," 306.

[115] Schwarcz, *The Emperor's Beard*, 249-250.

slavery was to increase the supply of free labor and gradually emancipate the slaves.[116]

Stimulated by trading partner Great Britain's antislavery activities in the 1820s and 1830s, Brazil had outlawed the slave trade in 1850 with the hope that eventually the institution would be unable to sustain itself.[117] As the result of the large-scale emancipation of United States slaves during the Civil War, antislavery efforts in Brazil were also encouraged. Yet the American example of turmoil and political conflict became a lesson to avoid concerning the danger of immediate and universal emancipation. After increasing impatience with the process, José Maria da Silva Paranhos do Rio Branco introduced a bill for the gradual emancipation of slaves that was adopted on September 28, 1871. The *Lei do Ventre Livre*—or the Law of the Free Womb—was a natural compliment to the *Queiróz* Law and provided that all offspring of female slaves would be free.[118] Although this measure seemingly guaranteed the abolition of slavery in an estimated forty or fifty years, the Rio Branco Law as it became known, contained ambiguities in language that significantly weakened its intent. The law in part read, "All children born of slave women in the empire, after the date of this law, shall be free;" however,

---

[116] Dom Pedro II made it clear that he opposed the institution and that he favored a carefully planned gradual course to avoid damaging the country's economic interests and angering conservative planters. Strauss, "Brazil in the 1870s As Seen by American Diplomats," 311.

[117] William Law Mathieson, *British Slavery and Its Abolition, 1823-1838* (New York: Octagon Books, Inc., 1967), 240-245; and on the end of the Brazilian trade, Robert Conrad, *The Destruction of Brazilian Slavery, 1850-1888* (Berkeley: University of California Press, 1972), 20-27.

[118] Calogeras, *A History of Brazil*, 226-248. Stimulated by Great Britain's antislavery activities in the 1820s and 1830s, Brazil's *Queiróz* Law of 1850 ended the legal slave trade and promised an eventual end to the system through attrition. Mathieson, *British Slavery and Its Abolition*, 240-245; and Robert Conrad, *The Destruction of Brazilian Slavery, 1850-1888*, 20-27.

the text that followed provided for children to remain under their mothers' care until age eight. Furthermore, owners would then have the option to receive an indemnity from the government of 600 *milreis* (about $300), or to use the services of the child until the age of twenty-one.[119] Most owners elected to use the labor of these *ingenuos* until their twenty-first year. Neither the conservative planters nor the liberal reformers were pleased with the law, and corruption in the form of illegal sales of *ingenuos* as regular slaves and counterfeit birth certificates flourished.[120] Yet this flawed measure served to silence calls for abolition for almost a decade.

Brazil unsuccessfully attempted to spur immigration during the 1870s to supplement the labor force and offset losses from the Rio Branco Law. The imperial government offered prospective immigrants free passage, provisions for six months, and half the cost of building a house, as well as 160 acres of land priced at around a dollar per acre. Efforts to encourage significant numbers of immigrants were largely unsuccessful, however, following the experience of American southerners. European countries discouraged relocation to Brazil based on Americans' failed contracts and the prevalence of disease.[121] In the late 1870s, efforts to entice Chinese immigrants floundered amid charges that they would in effect become slaves. In what was intended as an economic statement that also revealed his social prejudice against Chinese immigrants, Hilliard commented to Council President Cansanção de Sinimbu in 1879, "If

---

[119] See, The Law of Freedom, Law No. 2040 of September 28, 1871, *Foreign Relations of the United States* (1872): 69-72. Dom Pedro II was away on one of his many foreign tours and the law was signed by Princess Imperial Regent Dona Isabel.

[120] Even the *New York Times* was critical of the bill in its final form, noting its many flaws. *New York Times*, September 29, 1871. Strauss, "Brazil in the 1870s As Seen by American Diplomats," 323-325.

[121] Strauss, "Brazil in the 1870s As Seen by American Diplomats," 349-350.

these people come into your country, you will never get clear of them."[122]

That same year, Hilliard reported to Secretary of State Evarts that the Brazilian labor shortage was worsening as a result of negotiations with the Universal Interoceanic Canal Company led by canal builder Ferdinand de Lesseps. The Brazilian government promised de Lesseps the initial labor of 15,000 African slaves to help construct his trans-isthmian canal under a lucrative brokerage agreement. Leaders in the Brazilian chamber of deputies believed that this arrangement would provide the country with an infusion of much-needed capital, but the exportation of workers in a labor-starved market only promised to create more shortages in the plantation provinces.[123]

The growing labor shortages and reduced profits that would result from a shift to free labor caused conservative planter interests to resist any further emancipation proposals. Slaveholders were reconciled to the fact that slavery's years were numbered, but they were unwilling to accelerate a process that they hoped would stretch out into the next century.[124] To further erode conservative support for slavery, abolitionists had to address concerns that an end of slavery would further damage the economy and create national instability.

---

[122] Hilliard to William Evarts, September 4, 1879. *Foreign Relations of the United States* (1880): 86. Hilliard's comments likely resulted from his perception of the large numbers of Chinese immigrants who were arriving in California, as well as Peru and Cuba during this period.

[123] *Ibid.* Ironically, as the United States was actively assisting white southerners' return from Brazil, it was advocating the migration of black Americans to Brazil in 1878. Congress directed the issue of free passports to "any colored citizens of the United States who may wish to go to Brazil to engage in work upon the Madera and Mamore Railway." See, "An Act Authorizing the Issue of Passports Free to Colored Citizens Going to Brazil," 20 *United States Statutes*, 40.

[124] Calogeras, *A History of Brazil*, 252.

Thus Brazil's emancipation efforts entered a dormant period for several years. A senator from the Pernambuco region, however, emerged to re-ignite the moribund movement. Joaquim Aurélio Barreto Nabuco de Araújo was a diplomat, abolitionist, and author from Recife, who had been born into the planter aristocracy. Although he came from a background of privilege, he developed a strong sense of liberalism and humanitarianism from his study of law in São Paulo during the late 1860s.[125] By the time Hilliard had become acquainted with Nabuco during his first summer at the imperial retreat in Petrópolis, the Brazilian had come to favor a full-scale propaganda campaign against slavery. Hilliard had been impressed with Nabuco from their first meeting in Rio de Janeiro, and it was clear that Nabuco also saw promise in developing a relationship with this American diplomat. Hilliard later recalled:

> Young, thoroughly educated, already acquainted
> with Europe, having been attached to the Brazilian
> Embassy at London; of splendid physique and
> captivating manners, a member of the Chamber of
> Deputies, and a statesman of high promise, he
> bestowed attentions upon me which were
> appreciated.[126]

Nabuco clearly saw Hilliard as a potential ally in reviving a discussion of slavery in Brazil. During Hilliard's first summer in the county, the young Nabuco probed the American's ideas on race and society. Hilliard recalled that "We

---

[125] Carolina Nabuco, *The Life of Joaquim Nabuco* (Stanford: Stanford University Press, 1950), 3-31. For the liberal influences in nineteenth-century Brazilian law schools, see Andrew J. Kirkendall, *Class Mates: Male Student Culture and the Making of a Political Class in Nineteenth Century Brazil* (Lincoln: University of Nebraska Press, 2002).

[126] Hilliard, *Politics and Pen Pictures*, 380-381.

were much together, meeting in society, and walking and driving day after day. . . . Ambitious, but unselfish, he devoted his fine powers to the cause of humanity."[127]

As early as 1870, Nabuco had been refining his ideas on the problems facing the abolition movement in Brazil. While in Recife in 1870, Nabuco prepared a manuscript entitled, "*A Escravidão*," offering numerous arguments for the end of slavery.[128] Whether from legal, political, or religious perspectives, Nabuco concluded that it was not acceptable for slavery to continue for another thirty or forty years.[129] Believing that the time had come to change society's perceptions of slavery, Nabuco wrote, "In this moment, death is no longer liberation."[130]

Led by Nabuco, a new and invigorated antislavery movement began to develop in 1879. Following unsuccessful attempts to stimulate the abolition movement through bills introduced in Parliament between 1879 and 1880, a frustrated Nabuco turned from legislative tactics to an already prepared political strategy.[131] The Brazilian

---

[127] *Ibid.*

[128] The work was an incomplete and unedited manuscript that would later become part of his significant study of the Brazilian antislavery movement, *Abolitionism: The Brazilian Antislavery Struggle.* See, "*A Escravidão*," Joaquim Nabuco Papers, *Instituto Histórico e Geográfico Brasileiro*, Rio de Janeiro, Brazil. Hereinafter, Nabuco Papers, IHGB. For Nabuco's persuasive work five years before the end of slavery in his country, see Joaquim Nabuco, *Abolitionism: The Brazilian Antislavery Struggle* (Urbana: University of Illinois Press, 1977).

[129] In Nabuco's legal argument against the institution, he frequently cited to the slave code, *Codigo criminal e a lei de 10 de Junho de 1835.* Joaquim Nabuco Papers, IHGB.

[130] Joaquim Nabuco Papers, IHGB. For a study of Brazilian attitudes toward the institution of slavery, see Carl N. Degler, *Neither Black Nor White: Slavery and Race Relations in Brazil and the United States* (New York: The Macmillan Company, 1971), 23-92.

[131] Nabuco's legislative attempts were overwhelmingly defeated by the conservative majority. Nabuco, *Abolitionism: The Brazilian Antislavery Struggle*, xx-xxi.

Antislavery Society (*Sociedade Brasileira contra a Escravidão*) was established on September 7, 1880, at a meeting of key leaders of the abolition movement including deputies, journalists, and professionals.[132] Nabuco, the society's president, organized abolitionist clubs that held meetings and recruited new members throughout the country. The society launched a monthly publication, *O Abolicionista*, and Nabuco adopted the creatively appropriate *nom de plume* "Garrison."[133]

The American experience with emancipation was so widely known that by mid-1880 Nabuco decided that the time was right to solicit the expert opinions of the senior representative of the United States in Brazil.[134] Keenly aware that controversy would stimulate nationwide press coverage for the antislavery movement, Nabuco planned to write an open letter to Hilliard soliciting his views on the nature of slavery and emancipation in the United States. Nabuco, of course, was already familiar with Hilliard's views and knew that he would respond.[135] Nabuco had begun laying the groundwork for Hilliard's involvement even before the creation of the Brazilian Antislavery Society. In an April 1879 article, Nabuco stressed the

---

[132] *Rio News*, October 5, 1880, *Biblioteca Nacional*. The symbolic date of September 7 was chosen recalling the date of Brazilian independence from Portugal on September 7, 1822.

[133] William Lloyd Garrison was of course the well-known editor of the American abolitionist publication *The Liberator*. For Nabuco's *nom de plume*, see Carolina Nabuco, *The Life of Joaquim Nabuco*, 367. Nabuco wasted no time in beginning the work of antislavery propaganda. In addition, he had the society's manifesto printed in English and French to offer the widest distribution of the movement's ideas. *Rio News*, October 5, 1880, *Biblioteca Nacional*.

[134] Carolina Nabuco, *The Life of Joaquim Nabuco*, 76.

[135] Nabuco had previously obtained Hilliard's agreement to participate. Carolina Nabuco, *The Life of Joaquim Nabuco*, 76.

importance of Brazilian-American relations, and the need for Brazil to be seen as a progressive trading partner.[136]

On October 19, 1880, Nabuco wrote a letter to Hilliard soliciting his opinions on how emancipation and free labor had affected the southern states.[137] Nabuco appealed to Hilliard's sense of humanity—in addition to his vanity—by thanking him in advance for his reply, characterizing it "as a service done to a million and a half human creatures whose freedom depends solely upon their owners being convinced that free labor is superior in all respects to forced and unpaid labor."[138] To further assist Hilliard in the points that the Society would like for him to emphasize, Nabuco included a copy of the manifesto of the Brazilian Anti-slavery Society with the correspondence.[139]

Hilliard likely did not have to think very long about whether to respond to Nabuco. He had been frustrated through much of his career by an inability to achieve the kind of long-term successes that he associated with the role of orator-statesman. The rancorous debates in Congress and a horrible war had left him feeling empty and unfulfilled. Hilliard craved redemption from a lifetime of personal and professional disappointments and he saw his participation

---

[136] *Rio News*, April 15, 1879, *Biblioteca Nacional*.

[137] The *Jornal do Commercio* and the *Gazeta de Noticias* published Nabuco's letter on October 31, 1880 and the *Rio News*, November 5, 1880. The correspondence was also widely distributed in Brazil as a pamphlet, *Biblioteca Nacional*.

[138] *Rio News*, November 5, 1880, *Biblioteca Nacional*.

[139] *Manifesto of the Sociedade Brazileira contra a Escravidão* (Rio de Janeiro: Reprinted from the *Rio News*, 1880). Also see, *British Sessional Papers: House of Commons* 85 (1881): 376-396. Francis H. Ford, the British diplomatic representative to Brazil who considered Hilliard a personal friend, reported much of the controversy by copying important press clippings and other activities to British Foreign Secretary, the Earl of Granville, George Leveson Gower. As a long-standing trading partner with Brazil, Great Britain had a strong interest in Hilliard's controversial activities.

as an agent for Brazilian emancipation as a cause worthy of his best efforts, regardless of the costs.

In his response to Nabuco less than a week after the Brazilian's letter had appeared, Hilliard outlined his ideas about the nature of American slavery, race relations in the United States, and the outlook for the future.[140] Hilliard argued that the subject of slavery transcended national boundaries and that the abolition of human bondage appealed to prevailing nineteenth century humanitarian sentiments for moral and social uplift. Hilliard would support the position of the Brazilian Antislavery Society and serve what he considered the good of humanity rather than present an accurate account of the dismal post-war life and labor in the American South.

Often Hilliard's narrative offered surprisingly candid descriptions of how he perceived post-war Reconstruction in America. Hilliard argued that the process had been designed to fail because of the forced or unnatural elevation to public office of former slaves who were encumbered by the heritage of centuries of bondage and restricted access to education. According to Hilliard, who himself had become a Scalawag Republican, "adventurers" from other states had sought to control the freedmen and had "encouraged distrust and hostility on the part of the colored people toward their former masters."[141] These circumstances had made it more difficult for black and white southerners to adjust to new social and labor demands. Hilliard claimed that although problems existed, never in world history have a class of people who had once been held in bondage behaved in such an exemplary manner after gaining their freedom.[142]

---

[140] Henry W. Hilliard to Joaquim Nabuco, October 25, 1880, Hilliard Correspondence, *Fundação Joaquim Nabuco*, Recife, Brazil.
[141] *Ibid.*
[142] Hilliard to Joaquim Nabuco, October 25, 1880, Hilliard Correspondence, *Fundação Joaquim Nabuco.*

Hilliard claimed expertise on the topic based on his position as a "native of the South, brought up and educated there, a slave-holder, representing for a number of years in Congress one of the largest and wealthiest planting districts and a section where slave labor was exclusively employed."[143] He challenged the stereotype that white men could not endure labor in a southern climate and that black workers lacked initiative and were "naturally indolent, thriftless, improvident, and utterly unreliable unless driven by the lash of a taskmaster."[144] His descriptions of post-war race and labor relations often drifted into overly optimistic descriptions of blacks and whites working well together through labor contracts and sharecropping. He described black workers as "cheerful and thrifty, supplying the best labor for the wide agricultural region of the Southern States."[145] Hilliard cited as evidence a productive and prosperous agricultural economy in which the largest cotton crop "ever made in the South" was produced in 1880.

At times, Hilliard's rhetoric displayed a decided ambivalence about slavery. Hilliard first condemned slavery in the United States as inherently evil compared to the Latin American institution. He described slavery as degrading to master and slave alike, but also in places defended the humanity of slavery in the United States.[146] He argued that when all the costs were considered, slave labor was much less cost efficient than free labor. In addition, Hilliard claimed that no labor shortages had

---

[143] *Ibid.*

[144] *Ibid.*

[145] *Ibid.* Hilliard's argument is similar to that of many "New South" leaders as well as some representatives of the black community including Booker T. Washington, who made similar statements during this time.

[146] For a comparison of slavery and race relations in the United States and Brazil, see Degler, *Neither Black Nor White, passim.*

occurred as the result of emancipation, because European immigration had increased to supplement the labor force. Emancipation in the United States, asserted Hilliard, occurred under the most unfavorable circumstances—it was sudden, violent, and universal. This would not be the situation in Brazil if the government moved immediately to prepare a plan to emancipate the remaining 1.5 million slaves. Hilliard proposed a symbolic date of September 28, 1887, to allow slaveholders to recover the cost of their purchases and then enjoy some profit from their current holdings.[147] Hilliard was not alone in his support for a gradual transition to freedom. Even the most passionate antislavery leaders such as the outspoken André Rebouças supported, within reason, a graduated plan for freedom as well as an eventual enfranchisement that would legitimize the new voters in the public's perception.[148]

Nabuco and the Brazilian Antislavery Society were extremely pleased with Hilliard's response and the public attention that it attracted. Hilliard was once again thrust into the limelight that he so thoroughly enjoyed. Nabuco's letter and Hilliard's response were published in almost every Brazilian newspaper. From October through December 1880, stories on the activities of the Brazilian

---

[147] The date coincided with the first gradual emancipation legislation (*Lei do Ventre Livre* or Rio Branco Law) on September 28, 1871. Hilliard could not know at the time how closely he had come to the actual date of emancipation on May 13, 1888. Conrad, *The Destruction of Brazilian Slavery*, 273. On an average, the break-even period for a slave was three years before the owner realized a profit. Hilliard, *Politics and Pen Pictures*, 397.

[148] Placing aside his hatred for the racism that he had encountered in supporting for Brazil, André Rebouças worked tirelessly for abolition as a founding member of the Brazilian Antislavery Society, the Abolitionist Confederation, and the Abolitionist Center of the *Escola Politecnica*, as well as being a strong supporter of the emperor, understanding him to be sympathetic to people of color. Leo Spitzer, *Lives in Between: Assimilation and Marginality in Austria, Brazil, West Africa, 1780-1945* (Cambridge: Cambridge University Press, 1989), 148-149.

Antislavery Society, Joaquim Nabuco, and Henry W. Hilliard appeared in almost every issue of the *Rio News*, *Gazeta da Tarde*, and *Jornal do Commercio*. The oversized bold headline of the November 15, 1880 *Rio News* read "Slave Labor—Free Labor," and was typical of the blanket coverage of the debate on slavery that was featured in most of the city's newspapers.

Conservative press reports sharply criticized Hilliard's letter and objected to a foreigner even entering the debate. Opponents of emancipation denied that the American experience with slavery had anything positive to teach Brazilians. The sudden emancipation of four million slaves had created social and economic instability in the United States, and conservatives charged Hilliard with offering a disingenuous version of events. Emancipation in the United States, the critics noted, did not stem from compassion for the enslaved, but came first as a war measure and secondly as "the act of a political party cunningly designed, by thus enfranchising a million or more of colored voters whom they could handle as they pleased, to maintain their political future control of the government."[149] Similarly, the *Gazeta da Tarde* pointed to the turmoil and violence, including the assassination of a president, that had followed emancipation in the United States.[150]

The *Jornal do Commercio* charged Hilliard with knowingly misrepresenting the situation in the United States, and claimed that Hilliard "unwarrantedly interfered in the domestic concerns of Brazil." The editor asked how anyone could believe Hilliard's assertions concerning profits of cotton production before and after the war as well as the fantastic claims of increased profits with free labor and the fictional account of harmony between the races.[151] Readers of daily newspapers were bombarded with articles

---

[149] *Rio News*, November 15, 1880, *Biblioteca Nacional*.
[150] *Gazeta da Tarde*, October 20, 1880, *Biblioteca Nacional*.
[151] *Jornal do Commercio*, November 5, 1880, *Biblioteca Nacional*.

either strongly supporting Hilliard as a friend of Brazil, claiming his letter to be a great humanitarian document, or offering a scathing criticism of his misrepresentation of the situation in America and meddling in Brazilian affairs. It was clear, however, that the Antislavery Society had achieved the goal of re-igniting the debate on the topic. Equally clear was the fact that conservatives were on the defensive. Following the enormous press coverage, conservative leaders offered to reopen the dialogue to include gradual emancipation laws in a transparent attempt to buy a little more time for the institution.[152]

Abolitionists emphasized the abuses that had occurred under the current laws. The Brazilian Antislavery Society highlighted the inhumanity of the institution by publishing long excerpts of the most severe examples from the slave codes.[153] The society reported more than six thousand documented failures or violations of the Rio Branco Law, as well as large numbers of Indian children in the Amazon Region being enslaved.[154]

The predictably harsh response to Hilliard's letter in the conservative press was hardly representative of the Brazilian people; many of them racially mixed and most supporting the abolition of slavery. Following on what they saw as the successful exchange of letters between Nabuco and Hilliard, the Antislavery Society scheduled a large banquet in Hilliard's honor.[155] Considering the previous weeks'

---

[152] *Rio News*, November 24, 1880, *Biblioteca Nacional*.

[153] *Gazeta da Tarde*, November 20, 1880. A series of articles describe the mission of the Antislavery Society and lists numerous officers and their duties. In addition, numerous examples of the harshest laws of the slave code were published—taken from the *Leis antigas o das ordenacões do reine*.

[154] On new evidence of Indian slavery, see *Rio News*, November 15, 1880. For failures or intentional violations of the Rio Branco Law, see *Gazeta da Tarde*, October 30, 1880, *Biblioteca Nacional*.

[155] *Sociedade a Escravidão, banquete offerecido as Exm. Sr. Ministo Americano Henry Washington Hilliard, 20 Novembro de 1880 no salão*

71

avalanche of press reports supporting his actions, as well as criticism and accusations directed toward Hilliard's role in events, he was somewhat reluctant to accept the invitation. Members of the Brazilian legislature had initiated official inquiries into the legality of Hilliard's remarks on Brazilian affairs and he was concerned that the State Department might recall him. Even Hilliard's supporters questioned whether his enthusiastic participation in the debate over slavery had overstepped the bounds of propriety for the representative of a foreign nation.[156]

Hilliard, however, feared that by declining the invitation he might damage the movement and "diminish the effect of my former utterance."[157] Hilliard insisted that the cause had "awakened my sympathy" and he enthusiastically attended the banquet leaving the outcome to providence.[158] Against the strong advice of many of his friends and colleagues, on the evening of November 20, 1880, Hilliard entered the grand salon of the *Hotel dos Estrangeiros* and received an exuberant welcome. Along the walls of the banquet room were the portraits of important men who had contributed to the cause of abolition. Hilliard gazed at the images of Abraham Lincoln, William Lloyd Garrison, and other "eminent men who opposed slavery," and was likely quite pleased at being recognized in such a manner.[159] The banquet was attended by more than fifty prominent Brazilian abolitionists and statesmen, and observers crowded outside of the opened windows of the banquet hall to listen to the

---

de honra do Hotel dos Estrangeiros (Rio de Janeiro: [for the society], 1880).

[156] Hilliard, *Politics and Pen Pictures*, 398; and Carolina Nabuco, *The Life of Joaquim Nabuco*, 76.

[157] Hilliard, *Politics and Pen Pictures*, 398.

[158] *Ibid.*, 399.

[159] *Ibid.* The portrait of Lincoln depicted him reading the Emancipation Proclamation to his cabinet. Conrad, *The Destruction of Brazilian Slavery*, 142.

proceedings.[160] Individual courses from the menu were named in honor of notable persons in the cause for human freedom such as, *"Bouchèes de Dame à la Monroe, Culotte de boeuf à la Paranhos, Poisson Fin à la Washington, Mayonnaise de homards à la Wilberforce, Jambon d'York à la Garrison,"* and *"Pudding diplomate à la Hilliard."* Each course, as well as toasts that followed various speeches were accompanied by *"l'Emancipation"* liqueurs.[161]

Many leading members of the Brazilian Antislavery Society rose to offer speeches on abolition and toasts to Hilliard. Describing the event to the *Gazeta da Tarde*, André Rebouças noted that the event was the first gathering of the "Brazilian Abolitionist Family" to "offer the saints' bread to those who live in the irons of slavery." Rebouças observed that while there were more than fifty abolitionists in attendance at the banquet, they represented in spirit the 1.5 million "brothers who wait for victory from the Brazilian legislature."[162]

In a lengthy introduction of Hilliard, Joaquim Nabuco defended the American's role in the debate because the fight for emancipation required worldwide support. Nabuco warned those who would delay the process of emancipation by alluding to America's costly and bloody experience. By speaking out against the institution, Nabuco argued, Hilliard acted as a friend to Brazil, providing a service to all, because "emancipation will triumph—it is not a matter of time, it's a matter of form. If not gradually, then it will occur immediately."[163]

After thanking Nabuco and the society for the honor of the occasion, Hilliard spoke of his admiration for Brazil

---

[160] Hilliard, *Politics and Pen Pictures*, 399-400; and *Sociedade a Escravidão, banquete, passim.*
[161] *Dinner offert a son Excellence M. Henry Washington Hilliard, Sociedade a Escravidão, banquete,* 23.
[162] *Ibid.,* 3.
[163] *Ibid.,* 5-6.

and his hope that the question of slavery could be resolved equitably and with as little pain to the nation and its people as possible. Commending the noble efforts of the men who joined him in the banquet hall, Hilliard placed their struggle in historical perspective and challenged Brazil's statesmen to rise to the occasion. After a brief attempt to defend his participation as acting in his personal rather than professional capacity, Hilliard closed with a toast: "Allow me, gentlemen, to propose a sentiment: The spirit of liberty—it cannot be subdued; like the central fires of the earth, sooner or later, it will upheave everything that oppresses it and flame up to Heaven."[164]

The newspapers were full of articles both supporting and condemning Hilliard's attendance and speech at the banquet. So widespread was the interest in the topic that prior to the dinner, the *Gazeta da Tarde* had published a lengthy biographical treatment of Hilliard and his career for readers who might be unfamiliar with the American at the heart of the controversy.[165] A conservative member of the Brazilian legislature, Moreira de Barros, asked in the chamber of deputies on November 22, "the meaning of the clear and manifest intervention of a foreign nation in an entirely domestic question." In another call for an explanation of the American minister's behavior, on November 25, sugar plantation owner Deputy Belfort Duarte con-

---

[164] Somewhat appropriately, Hilliard borrowed sentiments from his speech, "The Spirit of Liberty," to the literary societies of the University of Virginia in 1860. Henry W. Hilliard, *The Spirit of Liberty: An Oration, Delivered before the Literary Societies of the University of Virginia, on the 27th July, 1859* (Montgomery: Barrett and Wimbish, Book and Job Printers, 1860). See also, *Sociedade a Escravidão, banquete*, 9-12.

[165] *Gazeta da Tarde*, November 4, 1880, *Biblioteca Nacional*. The paper published an almost full-page biographical treatment on Hilliard that focused on his positive accomplishments. Two days earlier, the entire front page and most of the contents of the paper were devoted to the debate and controversy concerning Hilliard.

demned the attack by a foreign government on what "was perhaps the first element of civilization in Brazil."[166]

By late November the controversy was being fully debated in the legislature. The issue focused on whether Hilliard could separate his activities into personal and official categories to suit his circumstances. Hilliard's liberal party defenders claimed, "The Honorable Mr. Hilliard appeared at the banquet in a private capacity. What he said in his letter and at the banquet cannot be construed as anything but personal opinion."[167] The conservative response by Moreira de Barros asked,

> Who is not a diplomat? I know how difficult it is to make noble and high-minded people understand that propaganda given out under such conditions can go on growing until it becomes irresistible. But it is unfortunately so, as the plantation owners of the South of the United States found out too late. The same fate awaits the planters of Brazil if they are not aroused in time. The propaganda which today seems insignificant, tomorrow becomes more imposing, and if it is not blocked, it will cause the complete ruin of the present agricultural class, the glory and strength of Brazil.[168]

On November 25, 1880, the Brazilian chamber of deputies called a special session to hear charges concerning the intervention of a foreign minister in the empire's internal affairs. Certain that the emperor's liberal views toward slavery had something to do with Hilliard's involvement, Maranhão sugar planter Belfort Duarte proposed a resolution to call the chief counselor of Dom Pedro II, José Antônio Saraiva, to provide the emperor's views on the

---

[166] Carolina Nabuco, *The Life of Joaquim Nabuco*, 77.
[167] *Ibid.*
[168] *Diario Official*, November 22, 1880, *Biblioteca Nacional*.

incident.[169] The resolution passed, and the chamber of deputies posed the following questions to Saraiva:

First. Does the imperial government approve in general of the antislavery propaganda, and especially that which has been held in public meetings by means of political banquets, and a manifesto issued by a foreign representative?

Second. The United States Minister—did he appear at the antislavery banquet, held on the 20th inst., in his official or semi-official character, directly or indirectly with the acquiescence of the imperial government?

Third. In case of disapproval on the part of the imperial government of the conduct of the foreign representative, what steps do they propose taking, and, moreover, what line does the government propose to pursue in view of the illegal meetings on the question of the abolition of slavery?[170]

Saraiva responded that Hilliard's speech was not a manifesto, and that it was simply "the expression of the personal opinion of Mr. Hilliard on the question of slavery."[171] The Ministry's position, according to Saraiva, had always been that the Rio Branco Law could solve the question, because it can follow the gradual extinction of

---

[169] Saraiva Speech, *Diario Official*, November 25, 1880. *Biblioteca Nacional*. In 1855, Saraiva had argued that slavery should be abolished within fourteen years at the latest. In 1885, Saraiva would author the *Saraiva-Cotegipe* Law otherwise known as the *Lei dos Sexagenários* that provided for the freedom of all slaves sixty and older. Conrad, *The Destruction of Brazilian Slavery*, 222-224.
[170] *Diario Official*, November 27, 1880, *Biblioteca Nacional*.
[171] *Ibid.*

76

slavery and the progressive development of free labor, thus not damaging Brazil's economic progress. To the second and third questions, Saraiva responded that Hilliard appeared at the banquet in his private capacity, which had nothing to do with the approval or disapproval of the imperial government.[172] The distinction between Hilliard's official duties and personal opinions may have been as questionable as some of his assertions concerning race and labor in the post-war American South. It is fortunate for Hilliard that Duarte did not obtain the original copy of Hilliard's letter but instead relied on the press accounts of the contents. In addition to responding to Nabuco on official letterhead of the "Legation of the United States of America, Rio de Janeiro," Hilliard had the legation's secretary copy the letter in a legible hand with Hilliard's signature.[173]

Saraiva's speech was concluded with much applause and "*muito bem!*" congratulations by those in the chamber and in the galleries.[174] The saturation press coverage had stimulated public interest to the point that the chamber, the galleries, and even the corridors were filled with curious and enthusiastic onlookers.[175] Before the controversial exchange took place between Hilliard and Nabuco, the legislature had largely avoided the discussion of slavery. Conservatives argued that any abolition bill was in effect so dead that there was no reason for planters to fear Hilliard's comments. Indeed, a member of the chamber, Deputy Prado Pimentel commented on antislavery legislation, "Mr. Joaquim Nabuco presented a bill which, I regret to tell him, was rejected with general enthusiasm (laughter)." Nabuco

---

[172] *Ibid.*

[173] Hilliard to Nabuco, October 25, 1880, Hilliard Correspondence, *Fundação Joaquim Nabuco*.

[174] *Diario Official*, November 27, 1880, *Biblioteca Nacional*.

[175] Carolina Nabuco, *The Life of Joaquim Nabuco*, 77.

then added, "By all the slaveholders."[176] By December 1880, however, the Hilliard incident had focused so much attention on the issue that the conservative-invoked silence in the legislature concerning slavery was broken and there was no way to avoid discussion of it—especially in the press and on the streets.[177]

Pacing the floor all day at the legation waiting for news of the outcome, Hilliard was relieved when he was told of Saraiva's defense of his actions and that his fellow diplomats had all come out in support of him without reservation.[178] The exchange between Duarte and Saraiva, and the resulting swell in public support for the abolitionists' cause, showed how conservative attacks on Hilliard and the emperor's representative had backfired. The ensuing debate helped galvanize support for abolition and accelerated the emancipation process. Hilliard, however, also worried about Dom Pedro II's reaction to the controversy. Traditionally, on the first Saturday of each month, diplomats had short audiences with Dom Pedro II and Hilliard was anxious to see how the emperor would respond to him. When they met, the emperor drew Hilliard close to him, reporting in a muted voice "I have read your letter with great sympathy . . . and I wish to say something on the subject myself . . . I cannot do it here in Rio, but we shall soon go to Petrópolis."[179] Once again in the more relaxed setting of the mountain retreat at Petrópolis, Hilliard and the emperor took walks together and certainly spoke at length about emancipation—although the content of their discussions is not known.[180]

---

[176] *Ibid.*, 79.

[177] *Ibid.*, 78.

[178] Hilliard, *Politics and Pen Pictures*, 402.

[179] *Ibid.*, 396-397.

[180] A Portuguese member of the American consulate reported to Hilliard that the emperor asked a member of the council if he had read Hilliard's letter. The gentleman replied that he had not and the emperor

For years Hilliard had defended slavery as a legal institution knowing full well that it had become increaseingly isolated in the civilized world. He eventually decided that God himself condemned the inhumanity of slavery. Hilliard strongly believed that Divine Providence and his own suffering, especially the loss of two sons and his wife, the shame surrounding his remarriage and daughter's conception, as well as his inability to prevent the war, had prepared him for some worthy purpose. It was almost as if the theme was plucked straight from Hilliard's 1865 semiautobiographical novel, *De Vane: A Story of Plebeians and Patricians*, where after the appropriate level of suffering, the sinner is presented with an opportunity for redemption.[181] When he reflected on his long career, Hilliard's greatest sense of accomplishment seems to have come from his participation in the cause of Brazilian emancipation. Hilliard confided to a friend on learning that slavery in Brazil had been abolished, "that was the most heroic act of my life, and I desire it to be remembered of me while I live and after my life has closed."[182]

Hilliard enjoyed a pleasant summer in Petrópolis, and after a quiet spring spent attending to mundane official

---

responded to the man, "You must read it." Hilliard, *Politics and Pen Pictures*, 396.

[181] Hon. Henry W. Hilliard, *De Vane: A Story of Plebeians and Patricians* (New York: Blelock and Company, 1865). During the Civil War, Hilliard secretly married his deceased wife's best friend and nurse, Eliza Glascock Mays, with whom he had been intimate at some time during the latter stage of Mary Hilliard's illness. After news of Hilliard's secret marriage—and Eliza Hilliard's pregnancy—became known in Montgomery, Alabama, the couple abruptly moved to Eliza Hilliard's home town of Augusta, Georgia. Hilliard's family losses included two sons and a wife before his appointment to Brazil and another son shortly after his return. See Durham, "Henry Washington Hilliard," 189-190, 258.

[182] W.G.C., *Henry W. Hilliard: His Important Part in Brazilian Affairs, One of the Great Events in His Life* (Atlanta: Jas. P. Harrison and Company, 1888), 1.

duties, he requested a leave of absence with the intent to resign the post.[183] Hilliard's decision to leave Brazil was pragmatic. He could never match the experience of the previous year, and he had served his country throughout President Hayes' term in office. President James A. Garfield's inauguration on March 4, 1881, offered the opportunity for Hilliard to leave his post. Hilliard greatly missed his family whom he had only seen two or three times during brief leaves of absence in the almost four years in Brazil.

In June Hilliard received permission to leave, and he prepared to join his family in Europe for return to the United States.[184] Before leaving Brazil, Hilliard spent a long morning with the emperor at the São Cristóvão palace engaged in personal conversation without the formality of any official agenda. Dom Pedro II took Hilliard's hand and thanked him for his good wishes. On leaving the palace, the emperor and empress presented Hilliard with signed photographs of themselves of which Hilliard commented years later, "I still possess and prize these pictures."[185] On June 15, 1881, Hilliard boarded the steamer *Iberia* for Europe and took his last look at the Brazilian landscape. Standing on the deck, Hilliard absorb-ed every detail of the scene: "There stood the Sugar Loaf, the Corcovado, the Gavia[*sic*], lifting their heads in the clear light, their sides touched with tints of exquisite beauty. Never had I seen the city, the bay, the mountains, look so beautiful. A fresh breeze met the steamer and a swell from the ocean rolled in grandly."[186]

---

[183] For Hilliard's announcement of his permanent leave from the diplomatic post, see Hilliard to Minister and Secretary of State for Foreign Affairs, Pedro Luiz Pereira de Souza, June 9, 1881, *Arquivo Itamaraty*.

[184] Hilliard, *Politics and Pen Pictures*, 404.

[185] *Ibid.*

[186] *Ibid.*

Within eight years from the date of Hilliard's letter and the accompanying controversy, slavery in Brazil was abolished. Shortly after, Dom Pedro II and his family were forced from Brazil into exile in France where he died two years later.[187] One of the most prescient comments concerning Hilliard's tenure as Minister to Brazil can be found from Hilliard himself. In the young professor's 1832 speech to the to the Erosophic Society, Hilliard wrote the prophetic lines which still rang in his ears almost fifty years later, "When shall Erupides[*sic*] be forgotten, whose writings were so much admired, that his countrymen found by repeating them, they could loose their chains and free themselves from slavery? Or, who that loves art and genius, will cease to remember Phidias, who when banished from his own city, went to another, and won glory both for it and for himself."[188]

---

[187] A combination of the emperor's increased travel and neglect of the empire, and the post-emancipation gathering of planter support with a surge of republican enthusiasm, sealed the fate of imperial Brazil and ushered in the republican era. Schwarcz, *The Emperor's Beard*, 315-347. While Dom Pedro II was traveling in Milan, Regent Princess Isabel signed the *Lei Áurea* or Golden Law that simply stated, "Slavery is declared abolished in Brazil from the date of this law. All measures to the contrary are revoked." Gradual emancipation had been gradual indeed, and the law freed more than 700,000 slaves on May 13, 1888. Schwarcz, *The Emperor's Beard*, 314.

[188] Hilliard, *An Address Delivered Before the Erosophic Society, At its First Anniversary*, 7.

Brazilian Emperor, Dom Pedro II, 1885
Courtesy of Museu Imperial, Petrópolis, Brazil

Joaquim Nabuco
Courtesy of Museu Imperial, Petrópolis, Brazil

EXCHANGE OF LETTERS

JOAQUIM NABUCO TO HENRY W. HILLIARD

Sociedade Brazileira contra a Escrivadão,
Rio de Janeiro, October 19, 1880.

My dear Mr. Hilliard:

I take the liberty of sending to your Excellency some copies of the English translation of the manifesto of this society, and asking your enlightened opinion upon the results which the immediate and total substitution of slave labor by free labor has produced, and still promises to produce, in the Southern States of the Union.

No one is better qualified than your Excellency to speak—possessing as you do, not only the experience of a statesman who has played an important part in the events which resulted in emancipation in those States, but also a thorough acquaintance with their social and economic conditions—no one, I repeat, is better qualified than your Excellency to speak of the great revolution wrought in agricultural labor by the instantaneous liberation of the negro race.

The relations of the freedmen with their former master, their aptitude for free labor, the condition of agriculture under the regimen of hired labor, the general progress of the country since that inevitable crisis, are highly interesting subjects of study for us who will, like the planters of Louisiana and Mississippi, be obliged to avail ourselves of the very same elements inherited from slavery, and of the voluntary labor of the same race condemned by it to the cultivation of the soil.

There can be no doubt, after the late harvests, regarding the wisdom of emancipation as an economic measure for the reconstruction of the Southern States. Even Mr. Jefferson Davis has just acknowledged that the heritage of slaveholders has considerably augmented in the hands of free laborers, and that from this standpoint, abolition has been a great benefit to that section of territory where it threatened to become a catastrophe and permanent ruin. Unfortunately, however, it is impossible to convince the planters that their true friends are those who desire to give them a permanent, firm, and progressive base instead of this provisional one called slavery. The truth, when it appears, may come too late to prevent the ruin of the parties interested, and, as the sun, it may come only to illumine the wreck after the tempest. It is our duty, however, to enlighten the opinion of the agriculturists themselves by the experience of free labor in other countries, and to demonstrate to the country that only with emancipation can it trust its future to agriculture.

Your Excellency had a place in Congress by the side of Daniel Webster and Henry Clay; you belonged to the Whig party from which sprung the Republican party with its free-soil program. Your experience covers a long period, and your word is above suspicion. It is for this reason that I ask your full judgment upon the effect which the transformation of labor has had and will have on the wealth, well-being, and the future of the social community to which your Excellency belongs. Certain as I am that your opinion will have weight with all minds who see in emancipation the only problem worthy of arresting the attention of statesmen in countries which in this century are still under the opprobrium of possessing slaves, I thank you in anticipation for your reply as a service rendered to a million and a half of human beings whose liberty is solely dependent upon their masters becoming convinced that free labor is infinitely superior in every respect to forced and unremunerated labor.

With the assurance, my dear Mr. Hilliard, of my high esteem, I have, etc.

JOAQUIM NABUCO.

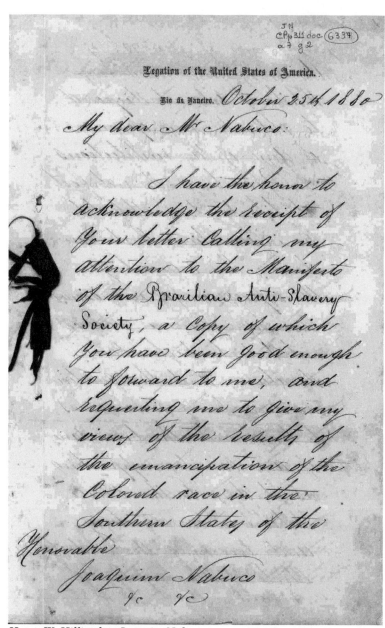

Legation of the United States of America.

Rio de Janeiro. October 25th 1880

My dear Mr Nabuco:

I have the honor to acknowledge the receipt of your letter calling my attention to the Manifesto of the Brazilian Anti-Slavery Society, a copy of which you have been good enough to forward to me, and requesting me to give my views of the results of the emancipation of the Colored race in the Southern States of the

Honorable

Joaquim Nabuco

&c &c

Henry W. Hilliard to Joaquim Nabuco
Courtesy Fundação Joaquim Nabuco, Recife, Brazil

HENRY W. HILLIARD TO JOAQUIM NABUCO

Legation of the United States, Rio de Janeiro, October 25, 1880.

My Dear Mr. Nabuco:

I have the honor to acknowledge the receipt of your letter calling my attention to the manifesto of the Brazilian Anti-Slavery Society, a copy of which you have been good enough to forward to me, and requesting me to give my views of the results of the emancipation of the colored race in the Southern States of the Union.

While I am not disposed to obtrude my opinions of any of the institutions of Brazil, I do not feel at liberty to withhold the information that you desire, the request for the expression of my views coming from a source entitled to high consideration, and the question involved being so large as to transcend the boundaries of any country, appealing, as it does to the civilization of our century, and touching the widest circle of humanity. I recall the sentiment of a classical poet, expressed in one of his plays:

**"I am a man,
And I cannot be indifferent to anything
That affects humanity."**

When that line was uttered in a Roman theatre, filled with a people accustomed to witness the fierce sports of the Coliseum, it was received with thunders of applause. Such a sentiment can never lose its force with the advanced civilization of the world.

Slavery in the United States is to be distinguished from that which existed in other countries growing out of the patriarchal authority, or resulting from capture in war, or punishment for crime. It was part of a commercial system that did not content itself with ordinary objects of trade, but took hold of the African race as offering a tempting reward for enterprise, and promising a speedy return for the outlay of capital—at once atrocious, reckless, and selfish. For two centuries this inhuman trade was carried on, without re-monstrance or even criticism. The American continent offered the best market in the world for the sale of slaves. Slavery was planted on the soil of the English colonies, stretching from New England to Georgia. When the colonies threw off their allegiance to England they were independent of each other, but they made common cause, and at the close of the war they became free and inde-pendent States. When it became necessary to form a more perfect union, the several States met in convention, General Washington presiding, and they established a national government. The Constitution conferred upon this govern-ment great powers, powers supreme and sovereign. But the powers not delegated to the United States by the Con-stitution, nor prohibited by it to the States, were reserved to the States respectively or to the people. The national government had no jurisdiction over the domestic insti-tutions of the States. Slavery was left under the absolute control of each State where it existed. It was the object of the framers of the Constitution to leave slavery in the States where it existed, without adding any sanction to it, to be disposed of by each State without reference to the others.

In the course of time a strong hostility to slavery began to exhibit itself in some of the communities of the North. Attempts were made to determine the territorial bounds to which slavery should be confined within the United States, and into this discussion the distribution of power and sectional aggrandizement largely entered. Upon the application of Missouri—a new State in which slavery existed, organized out of a territory belonging to the United States—for admission to the Union, a fierce contest ensued which was happily compromised by the fixing of the line of 36-30, and the territory north as free territory. The tranquility of the Union was undisturbed for some years, but upon the acquisition of new territory at the close of the war with Mexico the formidable question of the exclusion of slavery from it was revived. A powerful free-soil party was organized—a party that disclaimed any purpose to interfere with slavery in the States, but which demanded its exclusion from all the territory lying outside of the limits of any particular State. This party attracted to its ranks some of the ablest statesmen, who had, up to this crisis, ranged themselves under the banner of the Whig and Democratic parties. In 1860 the last great political battle was fought in which the old parties appeared in the field. The free-soil party triumphed. It bore its chosen leader, Mr. Lincoln, into the presidency.

Many of the leading men of the South insisted that the institutions of that section had been brought under the ban of the national government, that the Southern States could no longer look to it for protection, that the objects for which the Union was formed were disregarded, and that the time had come for seceding from it as a peaceful solution of a contest hopeless of adjustment. A large body of Southern statesmen dissented from that view. I was one of the number who believed that all the great interests of the South were far safer within the Union than they could be outside of it. I had some time before said in my place in Congress that the whole civilized world was against slavery, that it was protected only by the bulwark of the Union, and that we could already feel the spray of the billows that dashed against that barrier. But the hour had struck; the crisis had arrived; revolution was inevitable.

The great civil war that ensued shook the Union to its foundations; but it stood, for it was founded upon a rock. It is too early to write the history of that great struggle, a drama in which many who bore a part are still living. The national government triumphed, and slavery was immediately abolished throughout the United States. But it should be distinctly understood that war was not made on the part of the North to abolish slavery, nor on the part of the South to perpetuate it. It is impossible to comprehend the real significance of the question as to the results of emancipation, and the condition of the colored people in the South, without glancing at this historical review of the causes that produced a change unparalleled in the annals of the world, in the domestic and economic condition of a great section of the Union. These causes did not immediately cease to act after the convulsion had ended. Long after the storm has swept the ocean, its billows dash against the shore, and the ships that spread their sails upon its heaving bosom are driven far out of their course. Unhappily, the great quarrel originated in the relations of the Southern States to the Union, became a sectional issue, and it continued to influence the status of the colored race after emancipation had been accomplished. Political considera-tions continued to influence the settlement of a great social and economic question. In the language of Lord Bacon, "it was impossible to look at it in a dry light."

It was supposed, when the war was ended, that the freedmen of the South could not be entrusted to the control of their late masters. Measures were adopted for their protection. Not only were they admitted to equality under the laws, but political privileges were immediately conferred upon them. At the same time, the leading statesmen of the South were placed under disabilities. The anomalous spectacle was presented of colored freedmen suddenly elevated to office, while white men, long accustomed to rule, were excluded from posts of honor and trust. Not merely were the slaves emancipated, but they were permitted to dominate.

Numbers of adventurers from other States found their way to the South who sought for their own advantage to control the freedmen, and, utterly without principle, they encouraged distrust and hostility on the part of the colored people toward their former masters. Of course, under these influences, it was some time before the freedmen adjusted themselves to their new conditions. Many wandered from the plantations where they had been accustomed to work, and sought employment in the cities, leading a migratory and unprofitable life.

But it must be said, in justice to the colored people, that never in the history of the world has a class, held in bondage and suddenly delivered from it, behaved so well. During the war the slaves were exemplary in their subordinate position; no attempt at revolt was made, and in many instances they protected the families of their masters, who were in the army, to repel an invasion which it was declared would liberate them. So, too, since the war there has been less insubordination, less violation of law, less disregard of the proprieties of life on the part of the colored people of the South than was ever known in the history of any emancipated race. And this people were not a feeble, degenerate, scattered tribe, but actually number 5,000,000, contributing to-day an element of strength in the Southern States.

Never in the progress of human society have the two systems of labor—slave and free—had so fair a trial of their respective advantages as in the Southern States of the Union. I have observed the results of both systems. A native of the South, brought up and educated there, a slaveholder, representing for a number of years in Congress one of the largest and wealthiest planting districts and a section where slave labor was exclusively employed, I observed the working of that system, conducted as it was with every advantage of soil, climate, humane and intelligent oversight; and I am acquainted with the condition of that splendid extensive agricultural region to-day.

It was really believed throughout the South that emancipation would result in the utter ruin of the planting States; it was insisted that slave labor was essential to the production of crops; that the cultivation of cotton, sugar and rice required regular, constant, reliable labor; that if neglected at certain seasons all the results of previous toil would be lost; that the planter must have such absolute control over the laborers as to be able to compel them to perform their tasks; that it was impracticable to secure the industry requisite for success with free labor—contracts would be disregarded, disputes would spring up, and at critical times work would be abandoned, bringing irreparable disaster. It was said that white men could not endure steady labor in climates where these profitable crops were made, and that the African race could alone be relied on to perform the agricultural work in the great fields of the South. The negro, if freed, would not work. He was naturally indolent, thriftless, improvident, and utterly unreliable, unless driven by the lash of a taskmaster.

Some persons, too, who seemed to be deeply concerned for the well-being of society and the interests of civilization, professed to fear that the setting free of such a class would disturb the order of communities, sensitive to any extension of privileges to the African race.

But, in the order of Providence, all these clouds that threw their portentous shadows across the heaven of the future have disappeared. Galileo was right when he said "The world moves." Never were the States of the South so prosperous as they are to-day. Never were the relations between the white and colored races so good as they are under the new conditions of life in the South.

President Hayes, whose administration has contributed so largely to the advancement of the prosperity of the country in all its varied interests, said, in a recent speech in describing the condition of public feeling in the Southern States: "Material prosperity is increasing there; race prejudices and antagonisms have diminished; the passions and the animosities of the war are subsiding, and the ancient harmony, and concord, and patriotic national sentiments are returning."

The negroes labor well, patiently, and faithfully, not only in the cities but on the plantations. They are more intelligent and trustworthy than before emancipation, and whether engaged by contract, or working for shares of the crop, the results are far more satisfactory than under the old system of compulsory labor. They are cheerful and thrifty, and supply the best labor for the wide agricultural region of the Southern States that could be secured. The largest cotton crop ever made in the South, estimated at 6,000,000 bales, has been produced this year chiefly by the labor of freedmen.

The freedmen lay up something for themselves, and constitute an important element in the increasing wealth of the South. In one single Southern State this property is estimated to be worth several millions of dollars. They have advanced in intelligence, and are regarded as valuable citizens of the commonwealths where they formerly labored as slaves. In Atlanta, the capital of the great State of Georgia, there is a prosperous university for colored students. Some of the most efficient and conservative teachers in the State were educated there. Its students number 240, representing ten different States, and forty-seven counties in Georgia. The trustees hold sixty acres of valuable land adjoining the college edifices, a splendid endowment, and besides other revenues, receive 8,000 dollars per annum from the State. The library already comprises 4,000 volumes. The spectacle presented by the Southern States to-day is one of peaceful, cheerful, prosperous labor; the slave driver has disappeared, the sounds that break the stillness of plantation life are the voices of a willing people engaged in work, which, while it enriches the planter, adds to the well-being of the sons of toil.

It is doubtless true that the system of slave labor in the Southern States of the Union was the most humane ever conducted in any part of the world. The planters, as a class, were men of a superior order, and they gave personal attention to the plantations. There were certainly occasional abuses even under that generally mild administration. It is impossible to provide against abuses under a system of absolute slavery. Where one human being has the power to control the labor of another, to assign his tasks, to order what his food and clothing shall be, to consign him to hard work in the most insalubrious spots, to take the products of his hands, to lay the lash on his back, to sell him away from his wife and children, to whip wife and child before his eyes, to become destiny for him, shutting out from him capriciously the light of heaven and the sweet pure air, it must be expected that the better qualities of human nature will at times be less powerful in dealing with the victims of such a code than the coarser and meaner lusts which have wrought so much wretchedness in the world. If Dante could have witnessed some of the scenes in these abject abodes of human misery, he might have deepened his description of the horrors in the "Inferno."

Fortunately for us in the United States, even the humane system of slavery which prevailed there has passed away for ever. The shadow upon the dial of human conscience must go back many degrees before any considerable number of men in the Southern States of the Union would consent to see slavery restored. To-day, not a slave treads the soil of freedom from the waters of the St. Lawrence to the Mexican sea, from the shore of the Atlantic, where the rising sun greets the flag of the Republic, to the distant coast of the Pacific, where his setting beams kindle upon its folds.

It is now clearly understood that slave labor is the dearest in the world. The money invested in the purchase of slaves, the expenses incurred in maintaining them, the charges incident to keeping them in health and comfort, the duty of providing for the infirm and the aged, require a large amount of capital, from which free labor is exempt.

But there are higher considerations than these: the responsibility, the deep abiding sense of conscientious duty, the obligation to acquit one's self well of the great task of compelling labor and of grasping all its fruits, the accountability for the well-being of dependent creatures— all this, viewed in the light that reveals all human affairs, must throw an ominous shadow over the places where the slave abides, and sighs, and toils in hopeless captivity.

Since the abolition of slavery in the Southern States of the Union, a movement in favor of immigration from other States, and from abroad, has been developed in the most satisfactory way. Heretofore, while the fertile lands and fine climate of those States invited settlers, they did not come, but made their homes in the West, contributing to build up great States, and covering the country to the base of the Rocky Mountains with abounding crops, adding, above all, to the material wealth of those commonwealths, the priceless treasure of an abiding, growing, prosperous, and happy people.

Now I observe with the greatest satisfaction that an English Colony of the best class is about to be planted in East Tennessee, one of the most inviting parts of the Southern country. It is under the guidance Mr. Thomas Hughes, M.P., an eminent scholar and statesman, who has displayed admirable judgment in selecting lands for the new colony. It is the first token of a happy future for the States so long wanting such settlers. Such a colony would not have been founded in Tennessee if slavery still existed there.

Emancipation in the Southern States was tried by every disadvantage to which it could be subjected; it was sudden, violent, and universal. The passage of the Red Sea seemed to be full of peril, but the enfranchised hosts passed over dry-shod, and the captivity was ended. It seemed to be better that this great transformation should be gradual, that both the white and colored races might prepare for the structural change in their relations to each other. I thought that this would require several years. Emancipation was not only immediate and universal, accomplished between the rising and the going down of the sun, but it was without compensation. Such a revolution in human society had never before occurred since men first began to gather into communities on the plains of the East.

Many Southern families were utterly impoverished. A new and terrible appeal was made to the noble qualities of Southern men, but they bore it well, heroically, grandly. And now that it is all over we would not recall the past. We do not speak of destiny; we submit to Providence. The mighty change that has taken place in our fortunes awakens in us neither regrets nor reproaches. We have turned our backs on the past; we look with courage to the future. The effect upon the white race at the South is infinitely better. Our young men respond to the appeal to their manhood; they address themselves to the tasks of life with energy and purpose. They have caught the spirit of our great poet, Longfellow's line—

"Life is real, life is earnest."

So, too, this deliverance from bondage is better for the colored race; they enjoy at once, without a lingering captivity, the priceless treasure of freedom.

I have read the manifesto of the Anti-Slavery Society with profound interest. The cause is set forth with great ability, and the appeal in behalf of the enslaved race is most impressive.

It seems that slavery in Brazil is already under the ban of imperial government. The law of the 28th September, 1871, adopted under the lead of your great and honored statesman, Visconde do Rio Branco, providing that after its promulgation no child should be born a slave in Brazil, announced that this great Empire had ranged itself with all the civilized world in condemnation of human servitude. The only question now is whether the million and a half of slaves in the country shall be still held in bondage, or be brought within the sweep of the beneficent spirit which prompted the grand act of the imperial government in behalf of human freedom.

Brazil is a great country, vast in extent, with a mild climate and fertile soil, yielding freely coffee, sugar, tobacco, and cotton, besides other agricultural products, rich with tropical fruits, abounding in valuable metals and precious stones, with a sea-coast 4,000 miles in extent. Such a country invites agricultural colonization. It need not distrust its future. It need not hesitate to commit itself to the policy adopted in the United States. With the extinction of slavery free labor will develop its immeasurable resources. The freedmen, already accustomed to its climate and its methods of industry, will supply the immediate demands for labor on the plantation. Gradually relieved from bondage, they will perform their tasks cheerfully, and ceasing to be a dependent class, not assimilating with the other inhabitants, but lingering in hopeless captivity, they will at once contribute to the wealth and strength of the country. Guided, trained, enlightened by the civilization that surrounds them, they will take part cheerfully in the industrial pursuits of the country—a country destined to be one of the greatest and happiest on the globe.

As to the time to be fixed for the full enfranchisement of the enslaved race, it is well to consult the experience of other countries in dealing with this important question. The ministry in England took up the subject as early as 1832; they proposed to inquire:

First. Whether the slaves, if emancipated, would maintain themselves, be industrious, and disposed to acquire property by labor?

Second. Whether the dangers of convulsions would be greater from freedom withheld than from freedom granted?

But before the report was made Parliament adopted an emancipation plan, and fixed upon a measure of apprenticeship of the slaves of four and six years, and voted moderate compensation.

The French government under Louis Philippe fixed ten years as the term, and added compensation; but the revolution came, and Lamartine at once signed a paper that set free the slaves in the Colonial possessions of France.

Seven years might be fixed as the term in Brazil for holding the African race still in bondage. It would seem to be specially appropriate, in selecting the period for the termination of slavery in the empire, to fix upon the 28th of September, 1887, the anniversary of the great measure which provided that after its promulgation no child born in Brazil should be a slave.

But the imperial government will treat this question under the lights that surround it and in reference to considerations which affect its own welfare. It is well constituted to guide the fortunes of this great country. Its history inspires confidence throughout the world,—its stability in the midst of convulsions that shook other states, its ruler displaying the great qualities of a man and a statesman, its Senate composed of wise, able, and experienced statesmen, profoundly versed in political science, its Chamber of Deputies constituted of enlightened gentlemen representing all parts of the empire with dignity and ability.

When the great measure of enfranchisement shall be matured and promulgated it will be hailed with the benedictions of mankind. May the day soon dawn. It will not only illumine the empire but will cheer with its light the remotest parts of the civilized world.

In the letter which you have done me the honor to address to me, you refer to Mr. Webster and to Mr. Clay as leaders of the Whig party in the United States, and to my association with them in Congress. I knew them well, and, though a much younger man, I enjoyed an intimate friendship with Mr. Webster.

Mr. Clay was a splendid impersonation of the qualities of an American statesman—bold, frank and ardent. He was distinguished for his oratory, powerful in the Senate, resistless on the hustings. He was Southern man, a native of Virginia, and a citizen of Kentucky, to which State he removed in his youth, and was its representative in Congress for many years. He favored emancipation in his own State, but did not identify himself with the abolitionists of his day, feeling bound to respect the provisions of the Constitution which gave Congress no jurisdiction, leaving it to be disposed of in the States where it existed.

Mr. Webster was a native of New Hampshire, but in his early manhood fixed his residence in Massachusetts. He did not commit himself to the measures of the anti-slavery party, being restrained by his respect for the Constitution of the United States. He won for himself the proud distinction of being called "Defender of the Constitution." No man surpassed Mr. Webster in the qualities that constitute a statesman; his imperial intellect, his large attainments, the tone of his character, the Olympian power and splendor of his eloquence, his personal appearance, the dignity of his manner,— all gave him an unrivalled grandeur in the midst of his peers. He filled so great a place in the country that his death was like the fall of a castle from whose battlements banners had waved and from whose embrasures artillery had thundered.

Both these great statesmen died before the crisis came that tried the strength of American institutions. If they had lived they might have averted civil war.

They were both leaders of the Whig party—a great, powerful, patriotic party embracing the whole country, and disdaining to bend to sectional influences. So long as it existed it was the great conservative power in the nation, protecting all its interests and shedding a splendor over the whole country. I shared its fortunes throughout the whole term of its existence. It gave way before the fierce sectional struggle that produced the war, but its surviving members still cling to its traditions and glory in its memories.

I need not assure you that you have my best wishes for your success as a statesman. You may not at once secure the accomplishment of your wishes, but you may live to witness the complete triumph of the measures which you believe will promote the prosperity and glory of your country. Few men are so fortunate as to live long enough to reap the fruition of their labors—labors faithfully performed for the advancement of their race. Every great political career has its vicissitudes, its lights and shades; the very energy that impels one to scale mountain heights may occasion a fall, but a true man will rise again to take part in the noble struggle of the forum.

Among the really great and fortunate men of our time Mr. Gladstone seems to enjoy the felicitous attainment of statesmanship described in Gray's fine lines:

"The applause of listening Senates to command,
The threats of pain and ruin to despise,
To scatter plenty o'er a smiling land,
And read his history in a nation's eyes."

May it be your good fortune to serve your country well, and to be appreciated for your honorable labors. The noble cause to which you have consecrated your abilities, the courage with which you have advanced upon your course, and the manliness with which you express your convictions, entitle you to the highest respect and consideration. The true object of honorable ambition is not success, but, as Lord Mansfield expresses it, "the pursuit of noble ends, by noble means." We must put forth our best efforts for the accomplishment of honorable and great tasks, but, after all, we must leave the result to the supreme ordering of Divine Providence.

I tender you assurances of my high regard, and I beg you to believe me,

My dear Mr. Nabuco, Your's etc.,

HENRY WASHINGTON HILLIARD

Brazilian Anti-Slavery Society
Offers a Banquet
In Honor of
The American Minister
Henry Washington Hilliard
November 20, 1880
In
The Grand Salon
Of
Hotel dos Estrangeiros
(in Cattete)
Rio de Janeiro
Typ. Primeiro de Janeiro.—Rua da Uruguayana N. 43
1880

Hotel dos Estrangeiros, Rio de Janeiro
Courtesy Biblioteca Nacional, Rio de Janeiro

BANQUET IN HONOR OF HENRY W. HILLIARD

Brazilian Anti-Slavery Society
Abolitionist Banquet[*]

From the time of Jesus and the Divine Master, the Saints of Peace and of Charity, of Liberty, of Equality, and of Fraternity are all gathered around this table.

For the first time, the Brazilian Abolitionist Family gathers today to administer the sacred bread of the Eucharist in favor of those who suffer under the weight of captivity.

This could not be a more solemn occasion.

The American minister, the venerable Henry Washington Hilliard, who during other times was a slaveholder and a southerner, practiced the sublime act of contesting those who would oppose the elimination as soon as possible of the shameful institution of slavery that causes much disgrace to this great and very loved nation.

This rare act of virtue moves all men of heart; the Brazilian Abolitionist Family wishes to convey their indescribable feelings of gratitude, and seeks to give the greatest proof of their eternal recognition of Minister Hilliard.

---

[*] The translated material in this section contains only minimal stylistic and clarifying changes. The reader should note the heavy sarcasm contained in language used in toasts to "praise" proslavery men.

This is the true significance of this feast today.

This banquet will gather fifty abolitionists: but with them will be in spirit, 1,500,000 brothers waiting for the delicious bread of Liberty . . . and with them will be the entire world, joining together for the victory of this auspicious commitment to Brazilian Democracy.

Ubi Spiritus Domini ibi Libertas . . . [Through this Spirit, God will liberate you.]

Through our own God of Justice, Equity, Liberty, and Equality, this brotherhood will be present to bless the feast of the Free and to benefit the Slaves.

Gazeta da Tarde, November 20, 1880, André Rebouças.

THE ABOLITIONIST BANQUET

As announced, the event took place on Saturday, November 20 in the Hotel dos Estrangeiros, a grand banquet offered by the Abolitionist Party in honor of the venerable American minister, the most excellent Mr. Henry Washington Hilliard.

Through the benevolence of Providence, this intimate feast of the Abolitionist Family gathered with great national joy to the cause of the Senate's vote, made some hours earlier, introducing the party of Liberty to the non-Catholics and naturalized citizens in the Brazilian Parliament.

It was with great happiness that this banquet was given.

DESCRIPTION OF THE ROOM

The room, in which the banquet took place, situated on the ground floor of this great edifice of the Hotel dos Estrangeiros in Cattete. It is an elegant, rectangular room, oriented east to west, the north face is adorned with two large mirrors, bordered with beautiful paintings representing Abraham Lincoln and his ministers Edward Bates, John P. Usher, William H. Seward, Edwin M. Stanton, Gedeon[sic] Wells, Salmon P. Chase, and Montgomery Blair, who heard the [Emancipation] Proclamation being read by the President-Martyr reinstating the freedom of 4,500,000 men.

The southern exposure of the room has four windows facing the garden, across the Rua do Senador Vergueiro, and was the scene of much activity during the dinner by some of the most notable residents of the beautiful aristocratic neighborhood.

The room is painted with beautiful green cane oil murals and adorned with tall window treatments in white transparent muslin.

The room was illuminated by three gas chandeliers above the table and by two bronze candelabra emitting a golden fire.

The table of fifty table settings had in the center a rich piece in the form of a castle decorated with the flags of Brazil and the United States and a large number of flowers in an ornamental stand.

The fine porcelain china with brilliant gold bands was placed adjacent to a setting of six crystal glasses for all types of wine.

When the guests, all in formal attire and with friendly smiles, entered the room it presented a beautiful spectacle, inviting the largest expression of joy and friendship.

Seating themselves at the table, the guests and dignitaries joined the most excellent American Minister Henry Washington Hilliard; Deputies: Counselor Saldanha Marinho, Joaquim Nabuco, Marcolino Moura, Joaquim Serra, Jeronymo Sodré, Counselor Adolpho de Barros; Dr. Nicoláo Joaquim Moreira, School Director Dr. Abilio Cezar Borges; Advisors: W. Lara de Tupper, Silva Mendes,

João Clapp, Marçal Pacheo and F.M. Cordeiro; Journalists: Dr. Ferreira de Menezes, Lamoureux, Angelo Agostini and Campos Porto; Drs. Ubaldino do Amaral, José Avelino, Alencastro, Sizenando Nabuco, Brazilio dos Santos, Vicente de Souza, Cardoso de Menezes and L.H. Pereira de Campos; Engineers: José Americo dos Santos, Derby, André Rebouças, Dr. Ezequiel Corrêa dos Santos, Castilho, Galdino Pimentel, and Abel Ferreira de Mattos.

Absent but sending letters of apology, were Drs. Gusmão Lobo, Ferreira de Araujo and Josédo Patrocinio; Deputies: Rodolpho Dantas, Barros Pimentel, Costa Azevedo and Entrepreneur James Gracie Taylor.

SPEECHES

Senhor J. Nabuco—Gentlemen, I stand in order to propose the first toast of the night, in the name of the Brazilian Anti-Slavery Society: to toast the honorable Henry Washington Hilliard, United States minister in this place.

When I sent to you our Manifesto, I thought of soliciting your excellency's ideas on the results of emancipation in the Southern States, and the response of your excellency was a service rendered to the cause of emancipation in Brazil. (General approval)

It could not be less, gentlemen, and that is why our society is publicly grateful.

What qualified Mr. Hilliard to offer a strong and unchallengedable opinion in this question? It was his first hand experience. (Approval)

For many years in Congress he represented an agricultural district, in which slave labor was used exclusively; he was a prominent member of the southern community; a slaveholder before the War, a Confederate soldier, and finally, representative of conciliatory politics and appeased by President Hayes, who, impartially appointed Hilliard to his post, a man who with great understanding of the cause, could talk about the economic and social evolution that was determined by emancipation in the United States. (Applause)

It is because of that, gentlemen, that I turn to the illustrious man from the States, for whom this feast is offered. Therefore, what did the opponents see in this notable and eloquent letter to this organization on his opinion of slavery? They soon saw foreign intervention in our internal affairs. How susceptible they are! (Approval) They do not have a precise knowledge of the United States, or Americans! (Clapping)

The representatives of an institution that for twenty years subjected our government to major violence on the part of England, of a class that courageously persevered in a pirated transatlantic traffic that morally disarmed the nation that was defenseless to resist the English traders when taking the entire African cargo in our territorial waters.

It was to them that the following two verses of vengeance grace the emancipation poetry of Castro Alves:

"Andrada! Rip that pendant from the air!
Columbus! Close the door of your seas![1]
(General applause and noise)

The truth gentlemen, it is too much. Because it is not clear that the Brazilian Army commander in Paraguay, the Conde d'Eu, asked by the government of that Republic for the complete extinction of slavery, and that by his initiative, slavery was abolished sooner, it is not clear that national opinion about that was revealed to the world in this most positive way: direct intervention. (Approval)

When the Zacharias ministry interpolated in the Royal speech reforming those who serve, did he not have to

---

[1] Antônio de Castro Alves is well known for his abolitionist poetry. The quotation is from his poem, *O Navio Negreiro* (The Slave Ship).

109

concede to foreign pressure? And what was that pressure? It was the appeal of the old European emancipators, such as the Duke de Broglie, Guizot, Montalembert, and Cochia to the humanitarian sentiment of the nation and the chief of state in favor of the slaves.

This moral support depends on the world's approval, it will honor us and we ask this. No more liberal cause was ever discussed in any country without liberal agitation in favor of this moral support. (Approval!)

Greece saw Europe supporting the cause; Italy provoked the same enthusiasm: wherever the elevated idea, nobody wants to be a citizen of a country where the struggle was denied to the heartfelt hopes of the race wanting to be free. If, in Brazil, we battle out of the view of the world and far away from world interests is precisely because we have not followed a policy that increases our contact with foreigners in our relations with the different world nations.

Do you therefore see, sirs, where does this susceptibility of our adversaries end?

To them, foreigners have only one way to get involved in the question of the element of servility between us: that is to buy the largest number of slaves possible. (Applause and laughter)

Not that long ago the unsuspecting authority recognized that a large number of foreigners owned slaves.

The right of a foreigner to possess a slave, a man who, now would be a Brazilian citizen and tomorrow would represent the country through the glorious vote of the Senate, today does not offend our sensibilities. (General applause)

When, however, these foreigners instead of showing their love for the country by buying slaves instead show you affection and love by freeing the slaves, violates the hospitality that is received and offends the countries institutions. Institutions of the country! Good institutions for those who are interested, they qualify as execrable, abominable, social afflictions, the cancer that gnaws at the

110

entrails of the nation. Because of this, it is necessary to know Mr. Hilliard: the difference that exists between us, and those slaveholders, is not in the manner of qualifying slavery.

At this point, in the interest of the proper cause, they banish us. (Chuckle) That is convenient for them. (Approval) While, therefore, we came to the truthful conclusion, but we did not complete it, and they had the opposite conclusion: the institution is certainly bad, but is a legacy in our country; what it means is that we have a conscience that slavery is a social crime, but this is not convenient to us, and by prolonging until the last profitable moment, taking from the institution, taking license to denounce it, like us, it softens the blow and deludes the opinion. (Applause. Very good)

Thus, gentlemen, when listening to certain speeches and reading certain articles, I can only believe that there is no difference between us and the slaveholders, that we all want the same thing, and until then, if you want to join us, emancipation would occur faster than we asked. (Hilarity)

There is no example of comedy like that. (Bravo, good)

And don't think, gentlemen, that emancipation is good for the slave. Far from it.

The slave is the happiest of men, happier than the Polish without a country, the Irish without a home, the English without bread, the German obliged to serve the military. In our provincial assemblies it is said that the slave is happier than our seamen. If they continue this propaganda in favor of slavery, it is possible that, tomorrow, many would like to become slaves. At least I suspect that the Coolies found enviable the comfortable position of the slave of a good owner. (Loud laughter)

With your attendance at this feast, Minister, you show well how distinguished popular sentiment is to our just outcry from our partners. You show that there is no belief that can sanction safe conduct over conscience, for having kept your great obligation, that no American could have abdicated—the free expression of your thought. (Bravos and applause)

It was done without violating our convenient position, not offending any susceptible country, and satisfying our United States friends, who represent North America in Brazil. (Applause)

When the Law of September 28 was passed, the Senate Chamber was covered with flowers: the previous American minister took an important part in our spontaneous celebration. We did not do anything but follow the example. (Very good, very good)

Certainly, minister, the country desires emancipation. The issue is not the time, but the form. (Approval)

If not gradual emancipation, then it must be immediate.

The time in which there will be no slaves in Brazil, is what cannot be prolonged by the bad will of the strategists who wanted to prolong the process.

Twenty years after the Law of September 7 of 1871, no one will have the right to complain of the state abolishing slavery. We will have had twenty years to understand that it was a national humiliation, a public hurt, a Brazilian disgrace. (Applause)

The day of emancipation will come, and this day has to be celebrated as the first national celebration in which all the sons of this country could equally participate, (Bravos, prolonged applause) and, this day, we worked to establish in an irrevocable manner and as soon as possible, we will remember all the pleasure that we had when it was our fortune to accept this challenge.

And it is an excessive demand to not sympathize with this movement that is beginning. And it is not necessary to know us. An old friend of Webster and Clay, experienced in public service, was among the shipwreck that was the Civil War. (Very good) He was a part of the largest rebellion that the world had seen, and was from the losing side. But when we reflect on your experience, we see you in Congress at Washington supporting with all of your effort Daniel Webster when, his strongly eloquent and prophetic words, imagined a great nation divided into adversarial sections and exclaimed:

Never liberty first and the Union after, but Union and liberty, now and forever, unified and inseparable. (Bravos!)

This was our political position, but dragged into the whirlwind of civil war, it should have been for us a dramatic and solemn time when we felt, confined by destiny of our State, identified with the fortune of our friends, our family and of our land, and those against this, rebelled against our country. In this moment this is what happened with Robert Lee, a heroic soldier of the Confederacy. With each victory gained by his military talent, his heart should have bled. He, the heir of Washington, condemned by his love of Virginia that was his little country, to destroy the larger country, the works of Washington and Lafayette. . . .

As, in the moment of prisoner exchanges in Richmond, the sword of General Grant, he should not have been grateful to Providence, in which was believed, having opposed a larger obstacle than could have been overcome, made the union of the country something superior to his genius and his bravery. As well with us, minister.

The day in which the conflict between the North and the South was decided, not in favor of two rival republics, but of one common nation, it is certain that this was a great joy in your life. (Applause)

And today, reconciling the South with the North through the political skill of president Hayes, he provided for us an elevated example of service for the country, what language does that speak to us! The language of a man for whom the past was a school and who was raised to say: the end result is the measure: the South benefited; the blood shed was the price of the liberty of five million men. We are confident with the result. (Applause)

In fact, minister, who will not recognize and admire the great morality of men of your temperament, having lost everything they do not lament, because it is for the good of the country and humanity?

And they do not want you, who approved of emancipation in the southern states, you associated with the heart of the peaceful movement, the legal movement, that was unfolding in this country in favor of the same cause! Do they not see that it is about the human race, about a traffic judged by the verdict of the human conscience, that it is now Brazil's turn, but the crime is the same with only one just end.

We want you Americans who approve of emancipation to excessively demand what has already been said. Being in Brazil like Benjamin Franklin was in France (bravos) on the eve of the liberal revolution.

Not considering the interests of the slaves and of abolitionists would be the same as asking Franklin to not sympathize with the works initiated by the spirit of the French Revolution. (Applause, very good)

No—you are right. Your name before was only known, but today is respected by all Brazilians: (applause) and is the name of a friend of our country, and will be even greater following this feast, in which the abolitionist party represented by the delegates gathered here welcome you because it is a tradition of our cause, to be repeated with the blessings of a million-and-a-half slaves and their descendents. (Applause)

Gentlemen, we ask you to drink with enthusiasm to the health of our distinct invited guest, the honorable Henry Washington Hilliard, honorary member of the Brazilian Anti-Slavery Society. (Prolonged applause. Long live! Hurrahs! Great sensation and vast joy! Rising, all the guests

114

increasingly shouted to the illustrious minister and to the Great Republic!)

HILLIARD'S SPEECH

Gentlemen:

In rising to make my acknowledgements for the very kind words which we have just heard from my honorable and eloquent friend, M. Nabuco, I must at the same time beg you to accept my warmest thanks in providing this splendid banquet as a mark of your appreciation of the sentiments expressed in my late letter in regard to emancipation in the United States.

It is not my purpose on this occasion to do more than to speak in general terms of the immeasurable advantages of free labor over a system of compulsory and unremunerative labor. It is a great social and economic question about which my own judgment is made up and settled. The experience of all nations teaches us that no country can enjoy the highest prosperity and happiness attainable where slavery exists. But I shall not enter into an argument in support of that proposition on an occasion like this.

Allow me to say I cannot feel that I am a stranger in Brazil. Long before I stood upon its soil and looked out upon its beautiful scenery (far the most beautiful I have anywhere seen) I felt a deep interest in the country. Coming from my own country to this, it seemed to me that the United States and Brazil were bound to each other by strong ties; that we were merely neighboring nations dividing between us so large a part of the American continent, and having great interests in common which we should develop for ourselves on this side of the Atlantic, without being disturbed by the struggles of the states of Europe. Your country, like mine, had thrown off its allegiance to a foreign power, and asserted and maintained its right to be free and independent.

More than this, in both countries a great system of constitutional government had been established. We have a day which, with every recurring anniversary, calls forth new attestations of popular rejoicing—the 4th July; and you have yours—the 7th September.

So, too, not a great while after our independence was accomplished, we framed a Constitution and established a national government, under which we have advanced to the highest prosperity. You, at an early day, adopted your constitution, under which you have made steady progress as a nation. One of the noblest monuments in the world adorns a beautiful square in your city in commemoration of the date of your constitution. In both countries there are great free governments, and both are advancing side by side to a prosperous, happy, and glorious future.

In my country we feel the highest respect and warmest regard for the Emperor of Brazil. When he came to us as a visitor he was everywhere welcomed; he traveled extensively; he saw our great cities, our broad plains, our growing States spreading from the Atlantic to the Pacific. And we observed him; we were impressed with his unostentatious greatness, the real majesty of the man, and the true dignity of the sovereign. When he took leave of our shores he left behind him countless numbers of friends, and we should be happy to welcome him once more.

In the views which I expressed in my letter as to the results of the enfranchisement of the colored race in the United States, I limited myself to a statement of the happy transformation in the condition of the people in the great agricultural region where slavery formerly existed, tested by an experience of fifteen years. As a man and an American I rejoice that slavery no longer exists in the United States. I confess that I should be glad to see it pass away from the whole world.

There are, gentlemen, certain great underlying principles which it seems to me impossible to disregard. You might as well try to disregard the laws of nature. And in applying these great principles we are apt to be misled if we yield too much to expediency.

Really there are some questions affecting human society to which you cannot apply considerations of expediency. The grand power of right asserts itself like one of the forces of nature. It disdains to yield to policy, and sweeps aside the obstacles that would impede the advance of civilization.

The mariner who would guide his vessel across the ocean does not lean over its side to observe the drift of the currents; they would bear him far out of his course. Nor can he always see the stars in the heavens; clouds may overcast the sky. But in the midst of darkness and tempest and the war of the waves, he fixes his eye on the compass that tells him his true course; the needle that trembles on its pivot, true to the power that attracts it, enables him to find his way in the pathless sea and reach the haven of safety. So in great questions affecting the destiny of the human race: to refuse to act because some inconvenience might result to us from our course, to look at the currents that drive us out of the true course, to refuse to look at the clear, unswerving line of principle, is to commit a stupendous blunder in advance. The great moral laws of the universe always avenge themselves in such cases.

I would not be understood to say that the conditions which affect the status of slavery in any country are to be overlooked or disregarded. Far from it. They are to be carefully considered. To accomplish in the best way and at the proper time any great work, we must study the proper methods to effect our purpose. But to refuse to listen to the teachings of history, to decline to survey the situation, to sit down with the selfish purpose to take no step for the advancement of the happiness of our race lest we should suffer by the change in the social condition of those about us, is what neither the philanthropist nor the statesman can approve.

Such a course makes one amenable to a moral law too powerful to be resisted. It is the beautiful expression of Hooker, that "law has her seat in the bosom of God, and her voice is the harmony of the universe." That law is irresistible in its force; there can be no harmony in the universe until right prevails everywhere.

Look to history. The nations in their march have shed a broad light upon the track of human progress. The mighty monarchies of the East have perished. The proud structures all over the world that dominated over human right, have gone down. Modern nations have sprung up; the principles of liberty have asserted their force; absolute power cannot lift its scepter in the light of the closing splendor of the nineteenth century. Public opinion to-day governs the world; it is impossible to resist it; it is making its power felt in all nations; it is more powerful than any government on the globe: its authority surpasses the fabled strength of Olympian Jove. It follows the sun in its course, and visits with its transforming power all places under the whole heavens. It will accomplish the enfranchisement of the whole human race.

I beg that it may be understood I do not permit myself to speak of the institutions of Brazil. In asserting my firm belief in great principles, I limit myself to a general statement. The application must be made by those who have the right to control the destinies of this great country—a country full of promise, with vast resources, and which will yet attain the highest degree of national prosperity and happiness. The time for the enfranchisement of the million and a half of slaves in this country requires much and careful consideration. The question is in the hands of wise statesmen, who will know how to treat it in all its important relations.

As I have said already, your government is admirably organized to dispose of all questions that affect the well-being of the country. The Emperor is known to be a great statesman, a profound student, who has enjoyed the advantage of personal observation of a large part of the world; your senators are able and experienced statesmen; your Chamber of Deputies is composed of gentlemen representing all parts of the country with dignity and ability, thoroughly acquainted with its condition and its wants, and competent to dispose of all the questions that affect its interests. You have a free and enlightened press. It is impossible to doubt that the important social and economic question, to which I have referred, will be disposed of in a way to advance the prosperity and happiness of the country. Such a cause as you advocate, gentlemen, must always encounter opposition. I dare say your great, honored, and lamented statesman, Visconde do Rio Branco, who has just gone down to a grave bedewed with the tears of a nation, found it no easy task to accomplish his statesman-like plan, providing by law that after its promulgation no child should be born a slave in Brazil. He encountered opposition, but he triumphed.

There is always a distrust of the successful working of any plan which proposes to effect important changes in the economic and social affairs of any country. The distrust is natural; it is to be respected; it is to be dealt with in the best spirit. But it yields to the irresistible force of enlightened public sentiment.

I am profoundly grateful, gentlemen, for this mark of your appreciation of the sentiments expressed in my recent letter; the opinions given with frankness, upon a great question affecting the destiny of our race and the interests of civilization, will stand the test of time; and I feel myself honored in being able to contribute anything towards the advancement of a cause which proposes to accomplish so much good for this great and interesting country. Of course

I could not intervene in the affairs of Brazil if I desired to do so; I entertain no such purpose. I state the results of my observation of the substitution of free for slave labor in my own country, and I trust to a generous construction of the spirit in which I have treated a great question which enlists the sympathy of the whole civilized world. I shall in the future recur to this occasion with an interest which time cannot chill, and cherish a pleasing recollection of one of the brightest evenings of my life.

Allow me, gentlemen, to propose a sentiment: The spirit of liberty—it cannot be subdued; like the central fires of the earth, sooner or later, it will upheave everything that oppresses it and flame up to heaven. (Applause! Very good! Very good! Repeated and prolonged bravos. The guests increaseingly offered great and warm vivas)

RESPONSES TO HILLIARD'S SPEECH

To Deputy J. Serra: Gentlemen—The abolitionist party disapproves at this time of those who are only found among the pensioners of Thezouro.

I see around me distinguished citizens of all hierarchies, and no one who does not live by his honorable work.

And in this party's future, is a better party that is not like that of the past. (Approval)

From the extreme north to the far south, many support our efforts, and it is in vain that a small group of agitators attempt to disparage us and inculcate us. We call ourselves—multitudes!

I remember with pride that the press, this great measure of public opinion, is all in our favor.

Here in the court, all the newspapers, with one exception, agree with our position.

In Pará, Maranhão, Ceará, Pernambuco, Bahia, and Rio Grande do Sul, they celebrate the beginning of the brilliant idea, which is our banner! (Bravos)

From São Paulo, whose language is the impregnable bulwark of our enemies, come to our language of excitement, comfort, and hope. (Approval)

Rejoice with our energy, or with the weaknesses of those who oppose us, and celebrate the abolitionist press of the country, particularly the deserving associates, who are present here, and who are so prominently represented! (Applause)

Senhor Ferreira de Menezes toasts the foreign abolitionist press represented by the editor of the *Rio News*.

Deputy Marcolino Moura: Gentlemen—After the enthusiastic toasts in which the abolitionist party, gathered here, offered to the illustrious Henry Washington Hilliard, in this moment attesting to the future through the difficulties and the present unrest, I come, with no offense to the modesty that evokes the memory of a great country to also toast. I want to tell you of the illustrious Brazilian, Visconde de Rio Branco, in which his name cannot be forgotten in this feast in the name of liberty. (Approval) And it is in the memory of his great soul that I want to toast. (Very good! Very good!)

Never sirs, around such general sentimental feeling by the disappearance of a notable statesman, will form a unanimous concept—from the idea that a great man will never die, to the contrary—he acquired more vitality that provides and sanctions the authority of the time from the grave. Providence reveals more satisfaction for the truth, rights, and justice!

Not only the feeling of prolonged lament of a race by the liberator of their sons; the trembling patriotic instincts of popular passions would come to feelings of want toward the grave of the Brazilian patriot, on which the dejected flag was hung; the memorable date of 28 September

121

1871—was also that of the eloquent voices of their adversaries, which obeying an unknown force, came to cancel their condemnation toward the benefactor of humanity. (Very good)

To the memory of the Visconde do Rio Branco, the justice of men was not slow, nor the lie of posterity, when in the middle of disheartenment and fatigue we hear your active and laborious cry—go ahead, persist—I will avenge you! (Bravo)

Celebrating your memory I raise this toast to democracy and the abolition of slavery, the ultimate right of all humans. (Prolonged applause)

Deputy J. Sodré said that if a number of current ministers were not leading the government, then they would be here at the banquet. (Applause)

Dr. Vicente de Souza toasts the abolitionists who are seated in the Chamber of Deputies. He was applauded unanimously.

Senhor Joaquim Serra—In the name of my colleagues who are present, and others who for imperious reasons did not attend this feast, I thank and welcome the illustrious democrat, who in the press and the popular platform, so bravely affirmed your individuality.

Gentlemen, it is important that the abolitionist deputies accomplish the duties that make them boast. It was necessary that the liberal chamber take the tone that we represent, so that in facing our party's commitment, some- one would respond to the thesis of our Manifesto.

But what would have happened to our cause if it was subjected to the management of the small factions?

What becomes great and invincible is the combined ef- forts of all parties of the country. (Very good! Very good!)

And thus we see in the Senate Senhor Jaguaribe and Candido Mendes, two conservative leaders, Saldanha Marinho, Menezes, Luiz Gama, illustrious republican names, and with them many others of all political factions and tones, working together, and fighting this battle against the slaveocracy.

Toasting, because according to all, men of good will support this cause: to the nascent abolitionist party of the country! (Applause)

Counselor Adolpho de Barros, vice-president of the Society, toasts to the cabinet of March 28, for two great services which were of service to the cause of emancipation.

The first, promoting the rise of the emancipation fund, and the second achieving the eligibility of those freed. Today is not just a regular day for us, because of this banquet in which the abolitionist party hosts the honorable minister of the United States, it is also a historical date by voting to accept the equality of political rights of the non-Catholics, naturalized immigrants, and the freedmen. (Applause)

Senhor João Clapp—Gentlemen, and the commercial class to which I am honored to belong, could not be indifferent to this civilized cause.

The cause of the liberty of slaves in Brazil, which is being so brilliantly praised by the honored American minister, and by all of you champions of the popular parliamentary tribunals, and the press, does not need my timid understanding of that which offers to the country the advantages of its next victory.

Namely, therefore, the great idea which gathers us here, I toast to the memory of the immortal Abraham Lincoln who pulled from captivity five million citizens who were stolen from the American Union and would have forever fallen but for this glorious martyr of liberty who overthrew this terrible treason. (Applause)

Senhor José Avelino (Judge of the Court) toasts to the Brazilian Anti-Slavery Society.

Senhor Joaquim Nabuco proposed a toast to England, and remembered its efforts to end the traffic. It had no other interests but to destroy the nest of pirates who traded blacks and to accelerate the end of the trading ships whose human cargo spoke to the interest of humanity. Moderates like Lord Aberdeen felt that this violated our sovereignty by putting an end to the wicked trade in Africans, but it was necessary to end it at any cost. The toast is directed to that small island obscured by the northern fog, whose strength resides in a race that settled, because of the increasing population, and its leaders founded far away great nations such as the United States, Canada, and Australia, taking to all of them Anglo-Saxon liberty which is the best that ever existed. (Applause)

Senhor M.E. Campos Porto—Sirs: humbly representing the Abolitionist Club in Riachuelo, and being part of the editorial staff of the newspaper that is energetically pledged to the complete success of the emancipation of Brazilian slaves; the newspaper in which the editor-in-chief, the illustrious and talented Dr. Ferreira de Menezes (very good), I believe, gentlemen, that I should affirm my ideas offering a toast to the hard-working and tireless Dr. Joaquim Nabuco. (Applause)

And gentlemen, this is not the first time that I have offered such deserved homage to the talent of this energetic member of the tribunal because in a different occasion, when the Chamber of Deputies denied the urgent need of this energetic abolitionist to establish his plan that was unfortunately annihilated by the political convenience of his adversaries, in that occasion, gentlemen, interpreting the sentiments of the Abolitionist Club, in Riachuelo, I directed to Dr. Joaquim Nabuco a manifestation that justified his good character, the greatness of his spirit, and his sincere dedication that consecrated the great cause of abolition. (Very good)

This manifestation earned the illustrious deputy a response that the Abolitionist Club proudly collected and that will serve to attest to the question of our aspirations, and perhaps, the great triumph, and the great glory to legitimize and confirm the rights and the justice of our cause! (Bravo)

I toast, therefore, to the continuation of this honorable tradition of the former Senator Nabuco: I toast to my friend Dr. Joaquim Nabuco. (Applause, bravos)

Dr. Americo dos Santos, magisterial Brazilian represented by Dr. José Avelino.

Senhor L. Tupper to the memory of Wilberforce. (Applause)

Senhor Joaquim Nabuco toasts to the political success of President Hayes with regard to relations with the Southern States. Understanding these political concerns demands that the man who today represents the United States in this court is an old Confederate. And the political reconciliation, the forgetfulness that erased the division between the old enemies and to make the Civil War a painful memory. In these politics it is expected that the future President, Mr. Garfield, will follow Mr. Hayes and we are hoping that there is no more a political north and south, but, that the parties can reach an equilibrium among all states and place the Union first, a unified country for all the Americas.

Senhor Marcolino Moura—I have in front of me a common friend, whose face is smiling, I always see him full of hope, challenging our sympathies. I will toast to André Rebouças, this hard working liberal and abolitionist who is loyally representing the science and glorious traditions of his venerable father. (Very good, very good!)

To André Rebouças—a friend of humanity. (Big and general applause)

Senhor Cardoso de Menezes—Sirs. The idea of the abolition of slavery in Brazil is not simply the patrimony of some citizens intimately connected by ties of patriotism, communicating the same beliefs, and rising in a saintly crusade against an institution condemned by the spirit of the century, and tolerated in our country, it can be said that

125

it is part of the condition of our social life and having your roots planted in the character of the Brazilian people.

The idea of abolition, you already know is the legacy of past generations, established in the great testament that began to develop in the beginning of this century, and proclaimed the extinction of the cursed traffic of Africans, and today, gentlemen, it is even more a true national aspiration. A solution for this eminent social problem is ardently desired by almost all Brazilians. (Very good)

Feeding the flattering conviction that the Brazilian Anti-Slavery Society suffered loud injustice and excruciating slander when it was bestowed on them the beginnings of this society in the form of an *ultimatum*—a cry for the emancipation of slaves—affirms that it is wrapped up with them that the claim of the revolt is its aim to conflagrate the country and to lie about the sincerity of its mission.

I believe, yes, this makes me full of noble pride that this patriotic institution represents in Brazil, and in the eyes of civilized nations, the role of emissaries of a generous thought that should occupy, and in fact, occupies the head of the world in which accomplishment is desired if not imposed by mankind's aspirations.

In this creed I adhere to this sacred cause that all of us defended and I happily associated with the highly significant demonstration of the abolitionist family with whom I am happy to belong. To the eminent representative of the United States of America, in Brazil, the most Excellent H.W. Hilliard, to whom I have the honor to toast now. For coming together with this valuable document to the history of the end of captivity in our land, the history in which pages only start to be traced but therefore they are already written with the shining language of patriotism and with the feathers of the sparkling wing of the angel of liberty.

It seems to me gentlemen, at this instant, the brilliant role of the nation, and the brilliant figure of liberty exchanges smiles of joy for this cordial and patriotic cohabitation, and around this table as if the horizons become indefinitely wider, still seems to me that a large group of slaves whose faces have been blackened by the unfortunate sun, gliding with thin threads of tears—tears staining and crystalline—are transferred into pearls and they seem to offer as first fruits of your profound gratitude, to all as the ones reunited here by the love of your sacred cause!

Well, gentlemen, in the name of those brilliant figures, in the name of the nation, in the name of liberty, in the name of gratitude of those captives, in the name of the ideas of the century and the destiny of humanity, we enthusiastically toast to the illustrious ambassador of the United States, the most excellent Mr. Hilliard, and through the example of the great country that he represents, serves as an incentive to the great aspirations of Brazil, and that the sun of the near future can illuminate liberty and equality of our two countries of America such as they could always receive the same bright sun that links us in a perpetual union.

To the most excellent Mr. H.W. Hilliard.

Deputy Sodré—to the unity of the country that through the abolishment of slavery will become stronger and more solid instead of destroying ourselves as threatened by the slaveholders. (Applause)

Senhor P. Mendes—To the venerable abolitionist Dr. Muniz Barretto. (Bravos and long live!)

Senhor J. Serra—Among the supporters who could not attend this feast; one of them deserves a special mention.

My political adversary, hardworking and admirable in the tribunal and in the press, who does not support our most inspired cause, and who is neither accustomed to mercy or to winning victories.

I toast to the distinct ex-deputy of Pernambuco, Dr. Francisco Leopoldino de Gusmão Lobo. (Prolonged applause)

Senhor Vicente de Souza—I rise at this time full of emotion and of fear. That the youngest and the least empowered should keep silent while waiting for the final outcome.

Senhor J. Nabuco—all of us here are equal. To raise a toast: it pleases me that I toast the vigorous militant and invincible legion of abolitionists in the Chamber of Deputies.

Heroes battling against adversaries, assured of victory; warriors, in any time you are fearful of supporting the crossing of arms.

And there, in that unconquered legion of fighters, I see the face of Joaquim Nabuco excited in his unshakeable conviction against, the arguments expressed in the words of the rancorous slaveholders like a torrent of lava destroying little black communities (applause); it is there that I face Marcolino Moura, the hero of the [Paraguayan] war and the hero of peace! (Applause for the speaker and for Dr. M. Moura)

He who listened to the mournful sigh of the nation, sacrificed fortune and well-being and he raised himself that his name was written on the glorious page of the major battles of South America, still continuing the glorious combat for the cause of the slaves, and, with the anointed word of philanthropy, defended the sacred abolitionist propaganda and reduced the ridiculous choice of occasional sovereigns to its true dimensions! (Acclamations)

And there is Joaquim Serra who many times, illuminated by beliefs of a great patriot (applause), many times castigating his adversaries who ridiculously claimed to be invincible, offering the most unprecedented proof of independence and of self-denial!

And there is sitting Jeronymo Sodré, my noble master, the fluent orator, energetic writer, and for all that we may say that he is the young son of a landowner who preferred an inheritance similar to ours, a life of prolonged sacrifice, of great works (acclamation), and rare dedication to the abolitionist cause.

Instead of a legacy of wealth by the sweat and tears of slaves, Jeronymo Sodré wants the poverty of a talented and modest professor of a university (approval), and finally, sirs, almost in the extreme of life's horizon, there is the unconquered soldier, the constant fighter, the untiring believer, who is Saldanha Marinho. (Bravo)

For this reason, I, a young man between you, no title but my effort for the cause of our brothers, because of this I toast the abolitionist party and the Chamber of Deputies.

Senhor Deputy Sodré—Son of a landowner, peasant like me, accustomed since I was young to closely face the hideousness of slavery, and since that time, I broke the laces that connected me to the deplorable past (bravos and applause), and I dedicated my efforts to the noble cause of the emancipation of elemental servitude. (Very good)

They say many times and with bitter censure, that we in the temporary chamber have gone further than our mandate; (not much approval) as for me, this idea is not accurate. Always in the popular assembly, the meetings of my party, the legislature assemblies of my heroic province, finally in the press, I attacked the existence of this social cancer, it is necessary and urgent to root it out quickly. (Much approval)

When discussing the Law of September 28—which I did not accept because I judged it to be incomplete and defective—it was many times censured by the illustrious statesmen who, recently deceased, left a great void in the Brazilian nation. (Very good and applause)

Gentlemen, sons of this immense continent surrounded on all sides by free nations and as much as we still today fight against the black wound, I could not, without humiliation, in good conscience answer the following question: "Because only Brazil offers so much wealth and natural resources, almost the same as modern Europe, and she will not be the exception to all Christian people, is she illuminated by the brilliant and splendid light of western civilization?" (Applause)

No, gentlemen, this question always humiliates the spirit, and for this reason and for always, I fight against the abominable institution of slavery. (Very good)

At last, gentlemen, I want to have the satisfaction of raising a toast to the young abolitionist party, which in this country will soon solve the problem that today is so complicated and represents a challenge to the common and systematic spirit. (Very good, long and big applause)

Counselor Adolpho de Barros, vice-president of the Society, toasts to the Chamber of March 28 for two great services rendered to the cause of emancipation.

The first promotes the argument of the friends of emancipation, and the second is to obtain the rights of freedmen. Today is not merely a date for us, because this banquet in which the abolitionist party toasts the honorable United States minister is also a historic day. It is historic because we vote to acknowledge the equality of political rights of non-Catholics, those naturalized and free. (Applause)

Senhor J. Sodré gives thanks and raises a toast to the patriotic and liberal chamber of March 28, adding that it is his conviction that some ministers would be here if not involved in government duties.

At eleven o'clock nearing the end of this banquet, I stand before the honorable Mr. Hilliard and propose a toast to the Constitutional Emperor of Brazil, who has already given his consent to the law of emancipation, and who knows the importance of his country and whose name is respected in the whole world as the name of my liberal sovereign. (Applause)

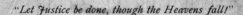

"Let Justice be done, though the Heavens fall!"

MANIFESTO

OF THE

SOCIEDADE BRAZILEIRA

CONTRA A

ESCRAVIDÃO

(Brazilian Anti-Slavery Society)

RIO DE JANEIRO
REPRINTED FROM THE RIO NEWS.

1880

Manifesto of the Brazilian Anti-Slavery Society
Bounds Law Library, University of Alabama School of Law

MANIFESTO DA SOCIEDADE BRASILEIRA CONTRA A ESCRAVIDÃO

(MANIFESTO OF THE BRAZILIAN ANTI-SLAVERY SOCIETY)

"Let Justice be done, though the Heavens fall!"

To the Country:

Three hundred years ago the first contract for the introduction of Africans into Brazil was celebrated, and for three hundred years we have existed in virtue of this contract. Slavery having been made the corner stone of our nationality, many still believe that if this foundation were to be destroyed the edifice would immediately fall. The coarse and barbarous superstition of slave labor has become to such an extent the creed of those who profit by it, that in their eyes one cannot be at the same time an abolitionist and a Brazilian.

The slave owner who cruelly beats or authorizes the punishments inflicted on these human beings for the sole purpose of increasing his own fortune; the irresponsible overseer who tortures pregnant women; the dealers who become rich with the trade in human flesh; the innumerable instruments of the infinite cruelties that go to make up what is called slavery: all those individuals who would be the disgrace of Turkey itself, seem very acceptable types of the old Brazilian customs and enjoy the advantage of not offending the patriotic susceptibilities of the advocates of slavery. Those, however, who wish to see Brazil associate herself with the progress of our century; those who feel that in giving the last asylum to slavery she isolates herself in a humiliating position; those who aspire to be citizens of a free country inhabited by free men and not divided between masters and slaves; these are held to be enemies to society and, whether called Eusébio, Rio Branco, or Pedro II, are always stigmatized as foreign agents.

Notwithstanding, however, the universal resistance opposed to the development of the idea of emancipation, it has never since the first advent of independence ceased to exist in the country and to show itself as one of those beacons that illuminate the whole horizon. The heroes of Pernambuco who in 1817 attempted our emancipation, had in view, as the founders of a free people, the abolition of slave labor. The patriarch of independence, the venerable José Bonifacio, from his exile in France, solicitous of the fate of the country he had helped to create, drew up a scheme for the gradual emancipation of the slaves which should be the completion of the national work to which his name is eternally linked. During the whole of our constitutional existence the abolition tradition has been perpetuated in our parliament, and in our annals one may see the vestiges of the constant revolt of the noblest and most enlightened part of the Brazilian conscience against the ignominy of an institution which is a violation of all the moral and social laws of the modern world.

All these manifestations, however, were isolated individual efforts until the day when, unexpectedly and while engaged in a foreign war, the government decided on initiating the reform of the servile element. The announcement of such an undertaking for which public opinion was not prepared, could not but produce a great sensation in the country, violently awakened from the moral insensibility to which the philosophy of those who profited by the traffic had up to that time reduced it. Act of a will which clearly was not the result of the general sentiment; the spontaneous initiative of the public powers in opposition to the interests that wished to remain stationary—the reform of the servile element nevertheless corresponded so well with the most enlightened sentiments of the Brazilian community that it became at once the aspiration of its directing elements. It was thus that, notwithstanding that the liberal party (in whose ranks the movement had met great opposition) had fallen from power, the engagement represented by words delivered from the throne did not fail to be honored and fulfilled by the Visconde do Rio Branco, to whom belongs the glory of establishing the Law of September 28, 1871, since which time no one is born a slave in Brazil.

The fact that the author of the legislative act that paralyzed slavery was the party which is everywhere the natural representative of privileged proprietary rights, of the monopoly of land and of rural feudalism, is a self-evident proof that when the country can wholly abolish it, slavery will find none but deserters among its best allies.

The law of September 28 was, however, a conservative law which respected superstitiously the interest of the masters; which guaranteed to them the property in their slaves until the complete extinction of the last; which did not modify what is with the master practically the right of life and death; which, binding the present generation to a captivity only limited by death, subjects future ones for twenty-one years to an irresponsible authority and to a systematic brutality, thus giving slavery a legal term of three-quarters of a century in which to disappear in the midst of the most terrible complications.

In the conditions the country was in when the blow was given, it could not perhaps have been more profound. The government could not require the representatives of conservative interests to yield at the first assault. It was clear, however, that a measure which was all in the future, could not be the end but only the beginning of the promised emancipation; that it was not a treaty of peace with slavery, but the declaration of war. Announced, however, as the law of emancipation, the act of September 28, 1871, gave rise to the belief outside of the country that Brazil had courageously liberated the million and a half of slaves which she still possessed.

Unfortunately, however, the Chamber of Deputies has by a solemn vote just dispelled the illusion of the whole world. Not only was slavery not abolished, but there is no wish to abolish it; and still more it is placed above the law. It has the privilege of being superior to the constitution. The liberty, the frankness, the publicity of the debates of parliament are very insignificant interests in comparison with it! The present slaves, a million and a half of men, can only hope for death, and the sooner the better! Parliament ignores them. Looking from its lofty height over the whole extent of the country, it can only discern the mansion of the master; it does not discover the quarters of the slaves. Slavery has ceased to be a problem, emancipation a reform. *The government does not think* of either the one, or the other. In the rapids that we are descending a helmsman is not required. The liberal government has become the trustee of slavery and promises to deliver the deposit intact, with the very tears, the very sufferings that constitute its wealth.

But will this be the definite result of the vote of August 30, 1880? No! This vote must be modified in the next session; free discussion must not again be denied to any partisan of the idea of abolition; the doors of parliament must open widely to it, if the liberal party wishes to be more than the submissive client of the great rural proprietorships, the agent of the stationary territorialism, which to the pro-slavery party is the true form of the social constitution. As the organ whose principal function should be the development and realization of the modern and civilizing aspirations existent in the most intellectual and progressive part of the nation, the liberal party cannot be the systematic negation of all liberalism, the officious and voluntary enemy of emancipation.

Indeed, for many years no reform will equal this in importance. An inheritance of the past, slavery is the still open ulcer of the old Portuguese colonization. Australia, which was a nest of convicts, eliminated this primitive element in the progress of her development and from a penal station became a great country. Brazil also needs to eliminate her primitive constituent element, the slave. She wishes to become a great nation, and not, as many wish her to be, a great slave barrack.

While a nation only progresses by the forced labor of a cast outside of the pale of the law, it is but an attempt at an independent and autonomic state. While a race can only develop itself in any given latitude, by obliging another to work to sustain it, the experiment of the acclimatization of that race is yet to be made. To the eyes of the traditional Brazilians, Brazil without slaves will immediately succumb; very well, this very experience has more value than a life that can only succeed in maintaining itself by the weakening of the national character and by the general humiliation of the country. If abolition be suicide, then a people incapable of subsisting by and for itself will do a service to humanity by having the courage to abandon to others, stronger, more robust and more vigorous, the incomparable inheritance of the land which they have not known how to cultivate and where they cannot maintain themselves.

But no! Instead of being suicide, the act of foresight as well as of justice which shall put a term to slavery will awaken inert faculties in the national character and will open to the nation, instead of the vegetative paralysis to which it is subject, an epoch of activity and of free labor which will be the true period of its definite constitution and of its complete independence.

There are indeed in the immense territory of the empire only sad and lamentable witnesses to the evil and fatal action of forced labor. Household slavery introduces immorality into all the relations of the family; it impedes the education of the children; it brutalizes the mistress; it familiarizes the man with the tyranny of the master which he exercises from childhood; it divorces him from labor, which becomes to him thereafter a servile occupation; it mingles the grossest superstitions with religion; it reduces morality to a convention of caste; it introduces inferior elements into the character which are antagonistic to all that make a man courageous, true and noble; it imprints on all who do not rise against it all the characteristics that distinguish a people educated in the midst of slavery from one educated in the midst of liberty. Field slavery, besides all this, covers the cultivated soil with a network of fiefs in which the master is the tyrant of a small nation of men, who dare not look him in the face; who are limited to the fulfillment of certain invariable obligations without liberty to give their faculties any other application; who are subject to an arbitrary regime of oppressive tortures; who are without any of the rights of men, not even that of founding a family, not even for mothers that of suckling their children; who are veritable agricultural or domestic animals nourished in vice and reared in degradation.

The nation that in the present century shall tolerate this regime with indifference, as immoral as it is barbarous, will be a condemned nation. We, Brazilians no longer, shut our eyes to this monstrous mutilation of man, to this systematic suppression of human nature in a million and a half of our compatriots of another race. Brazil can live without depending on the pitiless and iniquitous exploration of man by man. Hers is not a people which is usurping the place that another race would occupy with greater advantage to the American continent. Slavery has been for her only an impediment to progress; it is a tree whose roots sterilize the physical and moral soil wherever they extend.

Nothing so much offends the patriotism of the partisans of slavery as an appeal to the opinion of the world. No one can do it without being accused of relations with England. They have not yet pardoned her for putting an end to the traffic. Let them, however, say what they like; Brazil does not wish to be a nation morally alone, a leper cast out from the encampment of the world.

The esteem and respect of foreign nations are as valuable to us as to any other people. In the punctuality with which we meet our external engagements there is something more than shrewdness in paying to-day in order to ask more to-morrow; in that lies our self-respect. In such case our commercial honor is equal to that of other nations. This respect is not limited to the payment of our pecuniary debts. When our national honor was offended we went to the extreme of sacrifice to redress it. In such case our military honor is equal to that of other nations.

When a Brazilian takes our name to Europe; when the protection extended to European savants shows our intellectual culture; when in our external relations we appear in the light of an advanced, generous, and liberal country, our self-esteem is gratified and stimulated.

Under such circumstances then, how can an intellectual and sensitive people contemplate with indifference the degree of stagnation as regards the rest of the world caused by the maintenance of slavery? If to-morrow Europe and America were to join in a declaration making slave-holding equivalent to piracy, and subject as piracy on the high seas to the law of nations, we should be the only people to refuse our signature to such a protocol. Brazil, one of the young nations of America, to become the last defender of the right of barbarians to enslave, degrade, and mutilate their captives! Never!

The supposition that we can live in communication with the world, and yet remain indifferent to the moral blockade existing around us, is incompatible with the *amour propre* of the nation. We cannot blame the world for having advanced so far and in such a manner that we are no longer objects of sympathy, as happened with the United States of twenty years ago. We have no reason to complain because civilization has progressed so rapidly that it today considers criminal what, not long ago, was the normal constitution of colonial dependencies. Social ethics will not wait for our approval before becoming the general law of nations. Isolation is self-condemnation. The impulse of the nation is not to limit its sympathies to its own citizens without regard to that cosmopolitan feeling which scorns such exclusiveness. Its pride causes it to aspire to a partnership and a share in the work of the modern world. It wishes to figure in history, to have the right to raise its head on this continent, and to be neither a skeptic nor a cynic in its attitude towards the dignity of humanity. It is alive to the enormity of being a country of slaves, and is anxious to wipe out this blot by an act of self-sacrifice, justice, and reparation, in the firm resolve not to permit slavery to continue in undisputed possession of its remaining million of victims.

Whilst, however, the abolition movement has to struggle with minor prejudices, it encounters a serious obstacle in the union of the traditional healthy elements of the country with the systematic enemies of progress.

Among the many evils resulting from slavery is that of creating an abnormal union of all slave-owners, good or bad, humane or cruel. Those who act as the friends of their slaves, and the protectors of the freeborn children, make common cause with the butchers of their fellow creatures, and with the most infamous traffickers in human flesh that America has yet seen. Slavery creates an abhorrent class feeling among owners. The planter who manages his estates on an intelligent and kindly plan, who looks after the moral requirements of his slaves, who is the benevolent monarch of a people resigned to its fate, and whose wife and daughters treat the slaves as poor, necessitous and unfortunate; such a man will yet willingly associate himself with those who, regarding the slave as a mere beast of burden in place of a human being, buy him at a high price and subject him to such arduous labor as may in a short

140

time enable them to realize sufficient profit to secure them against any risk of loss. And still further, respectable landed proprietors allow themselves to be connected with slave-dealers from the towns and the interior on whose heads rests the blood of innumerable victims without one single drop having ever reached the conscience.

Against such a formidable array it would be useless to struggle were it not that it represents a state of things hastening to its fall, and a regime already self-condemned. So demoralized is slavery that the country will not long delay to reject its odious support.

Up to this point, however, we must fight a good fight, and for this purpose we have established the "Brazilian Anti-Slavery Society."

No members will be more joyfully welcomed among us than those landed proprietors who courageously and nobly desire to look the emancipation question in the face, and who, in place of opposing it, lend themselves to aid and direct it. The future of the slaves depends in a great measure on their owners, and our propaganda can only lead to creating sentiments of kindness and mutual interest between the one and the other. Those who from fear of the movement may be led to ill treat their slaves are those who, being naturally cruel, have no idea of justice. It is not the slave who will resort to criminal measures when a legal and peaceful emancipation is being entered upon. The sentiments of the slave for his master, his dedication, disinterestedness, loyalty, resignation, are of a higher order than those of the master for his *property*. Slavery has not yet succeeded in creating a hatred between the races, and when the master is just the slave repays him far in excess of any kindness he may receive. It is not possible that the peaceful task of enlightening public opinion and of accelerating the national will, with which all humanity sympathizes, should be hindered by the very beings whom it is meant to benefit.

What we have in view, however, is not only the freedom of the slave, but the freedom of the country; it is the development of free labor which has to take place under the tutelage of the present generation. We have no wish to renounce any of our duties, nor to repudiate any of our obligations.

It is the duty of the great majority of the country to impose upon the small minority interested in slavery its *ultimatum*, which shall be both just and inflexible. A powerful government representing the nation could without fear abandon the easy but inglorious attitude of indifference, and take into its own hands the direction of this movement, feeling sure that the country would accompany it with enthusiasm. The Saraiva cabinet unfortunately does not aspire so high; it merely aims at being an ordinary episode in our political life in place of being an event in our social history.

It is for this reason that the present movement is due to the unofficial elements of both parties. This society, for example, offers space to all; it is open not only to statesmen who can comprehend the plan and details of a gigantic work of social renovation, but also to obscure proletarians who hate slavery with the instinct of freeborn men.

To the Emperor we would say that there are a million and a half of his subjects who are outside the pale of the law, whose lot is one that finds no parallel in the civilized world, inasmuch as the proletarians of other countries are at least at liberty to emigrate, or otherwise to defend their rights and the honor of their families in the same manner as other men. We would further say that his long reign requires a crowning glory, and that this can be nothing else than the emancipation of the slaves. Let him remember that, without wishing to institute comparisons, we are an anomaly on this continent; we have slavery as a social institution and monarchy as a political organization, the result of which is that, in order to render a monarchy popular in America, it must accept the mission already fulfilled by it in Europe—that of destroying the feudal system and of liberating the territorial serfs.

To our constitutional parties we would say that they cannot be the supporters, the resigned followers, or enthusiastic advocates of a worn out institution which has been banished from the whole world; we maintain that the conservative party must see in the abolition movement the natural result of its own work, the recoil of its initiative; and that the liberal party will belie even the reason for its existence, the name it has assumed, the position it occupies, if once it places itself at the service of slavery.

To the republican party we would say that by the side of emancipation the republican cause is premature; that the skepticism which has led many of the purest and, as we have seen, of the very staunchest liberals to abandon the sterilizing organization of their party, would not be justifiable in regard to a movement so positive, so prolific, and so sincere as that of abolition; that the time has come for all who aspire to the founding of a free country, to unite around a common banner, which is the liberation of the soil.

We would say to the rising generation: children of slave owners, you must learn to rely no longer on wealth which has mankind for its basis; set no store on the chances of a property which would compel you to buy and sell human beings; repudiate all connection with a past which is thrusting itself beyond its natural term of existence; you cannot wish to be associated with the barriers which the advocates of slavery are endeavoring to raise in the path of emancipation. A man is not free either when he is a slave or when he is a master; but you ought to be free men. Future contemporaries of free labor, enroll yourselves in the ranks of the irreconcilable foes of slave labor; and you will thus have increased the usefulness of your life, by widening that space in which as Brazilians you will not feel the humiliation of seeing imposed upon your country the revolting bondage under which it is now weighed down.

Finally, we would say to the owners of slaves:—the law can deal with you in two ways: either by protecting you, or by calling you to account. You may take your choice. Slavery, of which you are the last representatives in the civilized world, can be extinguished from one day to another without any compensation being due to you from the state. It may be that the state has no wish to emancipate an entire race without regarding your individual interests. On you it depends to obtain this compensation in the name of equity, and to secure treatment as friends and as men of honor at the hands of the state. If, however, you oppose, as an actively adverse party, your *non possumus* to every reform; if you now place obstacles in the way of measures which would in the future facilitate the settlement of your legal claims without injury to your interests; if you become an insuperable barrier to each emancipation scheme, and recoil in terror from every step in this direction; then the blame will be yours alone, when the law, after so many frustrated attempts, shall like Lincoln with those Southern landowners whom to the last he would have spared, proceeded against you as if you were a belligerent and rival power.

Bear in mind that it is false that all this great slave population of the country is legally owned; the very registers, made with patent bad faith, would of themselves denounce the violation of the law of the 7th of October, 1831. After the traffic had been prohibited, the slave element of the country was still renewed by its means. There are employed in tillage innumerable Africans who have been criminally imported, and it is the offspring of these enslaved beings which constitutes the new generation of slaves. In its favor there does not even exist the excuse that slavery is a legal property: on the contrary, it is illegal and criminal on such an extensive scale that the simple revision of the titles to slave property would be sufficient to extinguish it.

The numerous party which does not wish to progress is composed of different shades of opinion. But even so, not one of them is so cynical and hypocritical as those who dare to call themselves *emancipators*, while all the time they are unwilling to do anything and reject both direct and indirect measures in favor of the cause which they profess to serve. According to them the country is not yet fit for emancipation and the slave must not be thrust on society, wild beast that he is, before he has been domesticated! But while they say this, there are no measures which terrify them so much as those which aim at giving a hope—however fugitive—to the slave, at instilling into him the aspiration to be one day free, and preparing him for his liberty.

The perils of agitation are great, but they arise more than anything else from that intractable resistance which is opposed to necessary reforms by an interested minority, a minority which unfortunately stifles the majority in its functions as the legitimate representative of the spirit of our institutions. Only let the rural proprietors become imbued with the idea of emancipation, and every Brazilian will bear his share in the sacrifice entailed by that forced cessation of their humiliating institution, which will be the natural end and result of those perils of agitation now so much feared. Let them have self-reliance, and let them by the courage of their initiative and their decision summon to their side, in place of the false friends who while they urge them to resist will be the first to desert them, the peace of their own conscience, the love of their slaves, and the gratitude of the whole country.

Let our enemies make no mistake: we represent modern rights. At each victory gained by us, the world will thrill with joy; at each victory of theirs, the country will undergo a fresh humiliation. Brazil would, indeed, be the very last among the countries of the world, if, having slavery, she had not also an abolitionist party; at least, the existence of such a party would be the proof that a sense of morality had not altogether deserted her. What we are doing to-day is in the interest of her progress, her credit, her moral and national unity.

By raising a war cry against slavery; by appealing to free labor; by condemning the fabric reared at such heavy cost upon the suppression of all dignity, energy, and liberty in the working classes; by proclaiming that no man can be the property of his fellow, and that no nation can with impunity build itself up upon the tears and sufferings of the race which has maintained it with the best of its blood and of its strength—by doing this, we only prove that we are worthy to belong to that free country, the foundation of which we are longing to see.

Many years have passed since the first stone of the great edifice was laid, but there is still time for us to leave our obscure names graven on the foundations of a new country.

Grounds of the American Embassy, Rio de Janeiro
Courtesy of Escola Alema, Rio de Janeiro

INDEX

98, 108, 122, 132-146

Broglie, Duke de, 110

Brown, John, 6, 11, 11 n. 32

Bryce, Viscount James, 2 n. 3

Byron, George Gordon, Lord, 4

Calhoun, John C., 32

Campbell, John Archibald, 6, 9

Campos, L.H. Pereira de, 108

Campos Porto, L.H., 108, 124

Canada, 124

Castilho, 108

Cataline, 11, 11 n. 32

Cattete, 17

Chamber of Deputies, viii, 62, 74-75, 77-78, 100, 119, 124, 128, 129, 136

Chase, Salmon P., 107

Chinese immigration, see immigrants, Chinese

Cicero, 4, 26

City of Rio de Janeiro, 58

Civil War, 53, 60, 66, 92, 108, 112, 125

Clapp, João, 108, 123

Classical training, Classicism, 3, 4, 26, 35

Clay, Henry, 4, 32, 86, 101, 112-113

Clayton, Augustin Smith, 23-24

Cobb, Howell, 33

Cochia, 110

Columbia, South Carolina, 18, 22, 24, 28

Confederacy, Confederate States of America, 3, 5, 38-39, 41, 113, 125

Congress, United States, 32-33, 68

Cooper, Thomas, 19

Cordeiro, F.M., 108

Dantas, Rodolpho, 108

Dante, 96

Davis, Jefferson, 32, 37, 38, 86

Davis, John C. Bancroft, 40

Degler, Carl, 13

Democratic Party, 5, 91

Demosthenes, 3, 4, 26, 35

Derby, 108

De Vane: A Story of Plebeians and Patricians, 79

Divine Providence, 18, 72, 79, 94, 98, 103, 106, 113, 121

Doyle, Sir Arthur Conan, 2 n. 3

Duarte, Belfort, 74-75, 76, 77, 78

Dunn, Ballard S., 53

Emancipation Proclamation, 107

England, see Great Britain

Erosophic Society (University of Alabama), 4, 35, 81

Euphradian Literary Society, 21

Euripedes, 81

Europe, 39, 115, 139, 143

Evarts, William M., 40, 41, 58

expatriates, southern (Confederados), vii, 42, 53-54, 55-56, 57-58

Fayetteville, North Carolina, 18

Fillmore, Millard, 35

fire-eaters, 21

France, 35, 100, 114, 134

Franklin, Benjamin, 114

"Free Birth" law, see Law of the Free Womb

Gama, Luiz, 122

Garfield, James A., 80, 125

Garrison, (Nabuco *nom de plume*), 65

Garrison, William Lloyd, 11, 11 n. 32, 72

Gaston, James McFadden, 53

Georgia, 3, 39, 42, 51, 90

Gladstone, William, 102

Grady, Henry W., 13

Grant, Ulysses, 113

Gray, Thomas, 102

Great Britain, 44, 48, 60, 90, 100, 109, 123, 138

Greece, 110

Guanabara Bay, 42, 43

Guizot, 110

Haiti, 4

Hayes, Rutherford B., vii, 10, 39, 41, 42, 50, 53, 57, 58, 80, 95, 108, 125

Hilliard, Henry Washington, voyage to Brazil, first view of Brazil, 1; Classical education of, 3-4; romanticism of, 3-4; as Whig congressman, 2, 4 , 8-9; as "crypto-abolitionist,"

151

5-7, 12; serves on secret "Committee of Six," 6; as Confederate soldier, 3, 9-10; scandal in wartime Montgomery, 10; becomes a Republican or Scalawag, 10; appointment as ambassador to Brazil, 10; anti-slavery activities in Brazil, 11-12; friendship with Joaquim Nabuco, 11-12; as "New South" booster, 12, 13 n. 38; returns to United States, 13; author of *Politics and Pen Pictures*, 10, 13; death of, 14 n. 40; early life and education, 18-34; diverse careers, 27, 31, 37, antislavery banquet, 72-78, 115-120; letter to Nabuco, 89-103

Hilliard, William and Mary, 18

Hooker, Richard, 118

Hotel dos Estrangeiros, 17, 43, 72, 106

Hughes, Thomas, 97

immigration, 61-62, 69, 97; Chinese, 61-62

imperialism, vii

ingenuos, 61

Italy, 110

Jaguaribe, Domingos, 122

James, William, 2 n. 3

Jefferson, Thomas, 8

João VI, 45-46

Kentucky, 101

Keyes, Julia L., 54

LaBorde, Maximilian, 19

Lafayette, 113

Lamartine, Alphonse, 11, 11 n. 32, 12

Lamoureux, 108

law, study of, 22, 29-30

Law of the Free Womb, (Rio Branco Law), 10, 60-61, 71, 76, 99, 129, 135-136

Lee, Robert E., 113

legal profession, 32, 36, 59

Legaré, Hugh S., 29

Lesseps, Ferdinand de, 62

Lewis, Dixon Hall, 20

Liberal Party, 11, 135, 136

Lincoln, Abraham, 38, 72, 91, 107, 123, 144

literary societies, 29

Lobo, Gusmão, 108, 128

Longfellow, Henry Wadsworth, 98

Louis Philippe I, 100

Manly, Basil, 37

Mansfield, William Murray, 103

Marinho, Saldanha, 107, 122, 129

Massachusetts, 101

Mattos, Abel Ferreira de, 108

Maxcy, Jonathan, 19

Mendes, Candido, 122

Mendes, Silva, 107

Menezes, Cardoso de, 108, 125

Menezes, Ferreira de, 108, 121, 124

Methodist Church, Methodism, 3, 24-25, 35

Mexican War, 33, 91

Mexico, 42

Mill, James, 19

Mississippi, 32, 85

Missouri Compromise, 34, 91

Mobile, 6

Montalembert, 110

Montgomery, 6, 29, 31

Moreira, Nicoláo Joaquim, 107

Moura, Marcolino, 107, 121, 125, 128

Nabuco, Joaquim, viii, 11-12, 13, 63-66, 69-70, 71, 73-74, 77, 78, 85, 87, 89, 103, 107, 108, 115, 124, 125, 128

Nabuco, Sizenando, 108

Nashville, 38

New England, 90

New Hampshire, 101

New South, 12, 13, 13 n. 38

North Carolina, 2

oratory, 21, 25, 26

Oregon Territory, 33

Ormond, John J., 7

Pacheo, Marçal, 108

Paraguay, 48, 55, 59, 109

Paraguayan War, see War of the Triple Alliance

Paris, 8

Parliament (Brazilian), 106, 134-136

Partridge, James R., 50, 57

Patrocinio, Josédo, 108

Pedro I, 46

Pedro II, 3, 46-47, 51, 52, 59, 76, 78, 80, 81, 116, 119, 130-131, 134, 142-143

Pernambuco, 134

154

155